A CATHOLIC STORY FROM THE CAMPS

THE AUSCHWITZ JOURNAL

.

Klára Kardos

Translated from Hungarian by
Fr. Julius D. Leloczky, O.CIST.

PARACLETE PRESS
BREWSTER, MASSACHUSETTS

In memory of my parents,
Gyula and Valéria Lelóczky
—J.D.L.

■ ■ ■

2020 First Printing

The Auschwitz Journal: A Catholic Story from the Camps

Copyright © 2020 by Cistercian Abbey, Our Lady of Dallas

ISBN 978-1-64060-488-9

The Paraclete Press name and logo (dove on cross) are trademarks of Paraclete Press, Inc.

Library of Congress Control Number:2019951174

10 9 8 7 6 5 4 3 2 1

Published by Paraclete Press
Brewster, Massachusetts
www.paracletepress.com

Printed in the United States of America

CONTENTS

KLÁRA KARDOS
1920 – 1984

FOREWORD

This book is an autobiographical sketch, written by a woman who never wanted to write her memoirs, who in fact never wanted anything but to live her life—her vocation—to the fullest as she saw it unfolding in the worst decade of the twentieth century.

When I met Klára Kardos, she was in her early forties. I knew her through correspondence. We were connected by our work of writing for a religious journal, which a group of Jesuits managed to publish in Austria and smuggled into Hungary. It was the only religious magazine in Hungarian that was being published for years without Communist control. Our intention with the magazine was to publish both the documents of Vatican II and literature about the council in Hungarian. An important function of the magazine was to support Hungarian priests serving various ethnic Hungarian parishes in foreign countries, some very old, some with a recently augmented refugee population. Most of the Hungarian priests needed intellectual and spiritual support, since they were new to the various countries in which they lived. There was some money available in the budget of the magazine for publishing books of theology and spirituality, three to four volumes each year. These were printed in Austria and smuggled into Hungary in small packages containing four to five books each.

Klára had no particular reason to become a refugee. As a survivor of Auschwitz, she automatically fell into the "anti-fascist" category, which protected her against harassment for her very devout life as a Catholic. (Klára attended daily Mass regularly.) But through the grapevine of the Hungarian refugees she learned that this enterprise of publications in Austria was in need of someone trained and experienced in journalism. With a degree in Hungarian language and literature, and some experience with a Hungarian magazine, she decided to leave the country illegally—that was the only way in the days of the Iron Curtain—and showed up in Austria, ready to work for the magazine.

In the summer of 1974, I spent six weeks in Klagenfurt, Austria, for a project. Our offices were located in the residence of the Jesuit fathers. The diocesan seminary gave me free room and board. I was working on a new translation of the Psalms of the Old Testament and preparing it for a new Hungarian breviary for priests and laypeople. In Hungarian there was no fitting modern translation of the Psalms. Such a task is a rather difficult job, requiring the knowledge of biblical languages and exegesis and the ability to write poetry in contemporary Hungarian. I experimented with this task for a few years such that, after being encouraged by some prominent Hungarian writers and poets, I undertook the translation of the entire Psalter. For this project I needed someone not only for secretarial assistance but also someone who could serve as an editor, a sounding board to critique my new text and ensure it conformed to the latest rules for Hungarian spelling and punctuation.

Klára was the right person. Her wide and deep knowledge of classic literature, including the Hungarian classics, amazed me. Her participation in the project guaranteed that our publication would not look like most products of emigrant writers, caught halfway between two cultures and several languages, and losing credibility at first sight.

She became a most valuable aide: her critique was honest, always well-reasoned, and both theologically and aesthetically sensitive. She was demanding, fast, and precise. She expected the same from me. It was clear that she knew how short life is: we never had time for idle talk or gossip, or even for relaxation.

She never talked about herself. I knew that she came from a Jewish family but was baptized as a child. Once when she wore a short-sleeved dress I detected a number tattooed onto her arm, a typical trace of time spent in a concentration camp. She was, however, unwilling to engage in conversation about her experience there. I learned of her experience in Auschwitz only from this very book, which was published in Hungarian after her death.

After the publication of the Hungarian Psalter, we stayed in touch. When I wrote my first biblical commentary in Hungarian, *The Letter to the Romans*, her encouragement and demands for limpid and precise style served me as if I were taking a graduate course in Hungarian composition. She encouraged me into undertaking another poetic adventure, the translation of the hymns of the Roman Breviary. The task was arduous, and without her help of line-by-line criticism and encouragement I could not have done the work.

I turned to her for help again when I began to translate a selection of religious poems by Rainer Maria Rilke from German into Hungarian. Rilke is, in the opinion of many, the greatest, most sophisticated, and most profound lyrical poets of all time. In the twentieth century no one wrote poems as Rilke did. Klára encouraged my first efforts of translating Rilke into Hungarian. The final result was a small volume of Rilke's poems reflecting his inner struggles for finding God. Rilke was raised as a Catholic, but all of his religious poems are brilliant aesthetic exercises of false religious sentiments, while many of his secular poems hide true yearnings to find God. In the middle of translating Rilke, in the summer of 1984, I had a chance to pass through Austria and see Klára once more. I knew she had cancer, but I did not realize that the therapies had failed and she had little time left. Our conversations were business as usual. The topics were language, translation, Rilke, theology, the Catholic Church in Hungary. Yet as we walked through the autumn forest to visit Klára's support group, a group of Lutheran ladies trying to live as a monastic community, I felt a sense of inexpressible sadness and the peace of a farewell, preparing a friendship that never had a chance to develop to become eventually a surprise gift waiting in heaven.

I spent the following months in Rome at the Biblical Institute working on a degree while recovering from my first heart surgery. I was fully engaged in all sorts of projects and yet deeply touched by the inexpressible lightness of existence. I received a short letter from Klára with her handwritten copy of a short poem by Rilke in German, a piece from his *Psalmenbuch* (Psalter):

Tear out my eyes, and I can see you still;
Plug in my ears: I hear you nonetheless;
With feet cut off to walk to you I will;
without my mouth, your name I still confess;
Break off my arms, and I, as with an arm,
Will seize you as I reach out with my heart;

Arrest my heart: my brains still throb and thud,
And if your flame into my brains should dart,
Then I will carry you within my blood.

(English translation by Jason Nicholson)

I immediately translated the poem with the correct rhythmic form and with rhymes and sent it to her for approval. I do not know if it reached her. I received a death notice soon after that: the cancer metastasized in her brain and she died.

I think of her often and exclaim with the words of one of my favorite (yet obscure) Cistercian authors, Konrad of Eberbach of the Middle Ages: *O quantos et quales fratres habemus in coelis!*—"O how many and how wonderful brothers [I should say friends] do we have in the heavens!"

—Abbot Denis Farkasfalvy, o.cist.

INTRODUCTION

Another book about Auschwitz after the thousands of accounts telling the horrors of the World War II Nazi death camps? No. This is a different story. This is the story of a young Catholic woman who saw the light of Christ even in the darkness of the concentration camp. This is a brilliant testimony of one woman's Catholic faith in the midst of the hands of an absolute evil power.

Among those interned in the Auschwitz death camp were many Jews who were actually baptized Christians, even cradle Catholics. Religious affiliation did not count in the Nazi assessment of who belonged in a death camp, and could not exempt one from their program of Jewish elimination: Non-Jews of Jewish heredity were taken to the concentration camp just as well. Thus, we can receive this account of an exemplary Catholic woman survivor who went through the hell on earth called Auschwitz with deep Christian faith.

Cold-blooded hatred knows no limits: it is able to commit the most unimaginable crimes. The dictionary defines the term *genocide* as "the systematic killing of, or a program of action intended to destroy, a whole national or ethnic group." The twentieth century could be called the century of genocides. Just to mention the worst ones in chronological order: the killing of Armenians in Turkey in 1915–1918, Stalin's forced famine called Holodomor in Ukraine during 1932–1933, the so-called Rape of Nanking by the Japanese in 1937–1938, the Nazi Holocaust slaughtering well over six million Jews from 1938 to 1945, the Cambodian genocide carried out by the Khmer Rouge regime in 1975–1979, the mass slaughter of Tutsi in Rwanda directed by members of the Hutu majority in 1994, and the "ethnic cleansing" in Bosnia-Herzegovina in 1992–1995. Of all these, arguably the most systematic, most methodical, and most meticulously organized mass murder, a veritable killing machine, was that of Nazi Germany, which was planned and executed to eliminate as fully as possible the entire Jewish population in Germany and other countries under Nazi occupation, along with hundreds of thousands of human beings of other ethnic groups.

These millions of people dying a deliberate, violent death (in many cases after excruciating torture) were not just statistics: each death was the irreparable tragedy of a unique human being created in the image and likeness of God, with a family of loved ones and with a circle of friends, often with tremendous talents, created for a happy life—truly beautiful human lives cut short by evil powers. We cannot find such evil in the animal world. Animals, including the most vicious predators, follow their instincts for simple survival: only human beings are capable of this kind of despicable depravity. Where does such evil originate? How does it spread in a society? How does it develop into a murderous rage? How did it start in Germany, the cradle of Nazism, in a nation considered Christian for over a millennium, with age-old Christian traditions, with a majority Christian population, with one of the highest cultures in the Western world?

Germany, after being badly defeated in World War I in 1918, was mortally humiliated and shamed by the Versailles Peace Treaty. Its territory was reduced, its armed forces were greatly diminished, and it was forced to pay huge reparations to the allied countries. With the abdication of the emperor Wilhelm II in 1918, a new democratic government was formed. Called the Weimar Republic, it ruled until 1933, amid tremendous difficulties. The Republic struggled with hyperinflation, increasing poverty, and extremist political groups both left and right organizing militias. The worldwide Great Depression of 1929 made the situation even worse, causing an unstoppable rise of unemployment. In this desperate situation, Paul von Hindenburg, president of the Weimar Republic from 1925, under pressure, appointed Adolf Hitler chancellor of Germany in 1933, after the Nazi Party won a considerable percentage in the elections; many voters thought that the Nazi Party would be able to solve the political unrest and the economic disaster of the country. The Nazis started a brutal campaign against the government and blamed all the ills of Germany on the Jews.

As the new chancellor, Hitler demanded a new election; by this action, he wanted to obtain full control of the *Reichstag*, the German parliament. Even before the election, the Nazis arrested leaders of other parties or curtailed their activities. On February 27, 1933, a Dutch terrorist burned the building of the *Reichstag*. This event meant the end of democracy in Germany: freedom of the press and other human rights were abolished. At the election held on March 5, the Nazi Party received 44 percent of the votes, and, with another party joining, they were able to form a government that quickly led to Nazi dictatorship. On March 23, the government passed the so-called Enabling Act, by which Hitler received the powers of a dictator. A formidable police and military force was built up, with various divisions (including the Gestapo and the SS), and the first concentration camps were established, the first of them being Dachau, near Munich. By this process it came about that, at the end of 1934, Hitler had absolute power as a dictator. Hitler's vicious anti-Jewish propaganda machine drastically increased anti-Semitic sentiments in Germany. Harsh legislation to curtail the freedom of Jews came into effect.

On November 9, 1938, in Paris, a young Jewish man fatally shot a diplomat of the embassy of Germany, an event that gave the pretext in Germany to start a violent attack against Jews. In a tragic event called

Kristallnacht (night of broken glass), riots broke out; businesses, homes, and synagogues were vandalized; Jews were mugged and killed; and over thirty thousand Jews were taken into concentration camps.

During the years of this increasing persecution, many Jews were fleeing from Germany into neighboring countries and from there to America. To stop the progress of escape, the Nazis effectively closed the borders so that, by the end of 1941, it had become impossible to cross over to other countries.

On September 1, 1939, Germany attacked Poland, and World War II began. Poland had a large Jewish population: over 10 percent, as many as three million people, were Jewish. From the beginning of the German occupation, Polish Jews were crowded into ghettos in which they lacked even the minimum of adequate necessities, and this consequently led to the death of a great many of them.

Atrocities against Jews increased even more when, in 1941, Germany attacked the Soviet Union and started the so-called Final Solution. Tens of thousands of Jews were systematically killed and buried in mass graves. In the outrageous Babi Yar massacre close to Kiev, over thirty thousand Jews were murdered in a two-day rampage. By the end of 1942 as many as 1.3 million Jews had been killed in conquered Soviet territories.

By early 1942 a whole system of mass murder of Jews had been set up. Six death camps were established in Poland, the most famous of which is Auschwitz. Jews were concentrated in many other camps too. Prisoners of these camps were used for slave labor or were transported to death camps. Most of the prisoners in these camps were Jews; the living conditions of each camp were so miserable that many of the prisoners died from the deprivations.

In every country occupied by Nazi Germany, first the Jews had to wear a yellow star of David on their clothing, then they were concentrated in ghettos, and later they were taken into one of the many concentration camps. Those young prisoners who were healthy and strong were not killed but rather transported to a forced labor camp to work up to twelve or more hours a day at a factory producing ammunition for the Nazi war machine.

In the death camps, new "shipments" of Jews arrived daily. At the camps, all their property and valuables were taken away; they were sent either to forced labor camps or directly to die in gas chambers, where their bodies were cremated. This is the reason for which this systematic operation of killing the Jews is called "Holocaust," a biblical term for "burnt sacrifice." It is estimated that about 3.5 million Jews were killed in these death camps. The mass murders were not limited only to Jews: tens of thousands of Poles, Germans, gypsies, and mentally ill were also victims of the Nazis.

Toward the end of the war, as the Allied military advanced and the Germans retreated, the Nazis forced the prisoners to march to other concentration camps; starved, they had to walk hundreds of miles in miserable footwear. Many of them died of exhaustion or were shot to death if they were unable to march any longer. Tens of thousands of Jews died in these death marches.

As the German military retreated and the Allies moved forward more and more rapidly into Germany proper, camps were liberated one after the other, some already at the end of 1944, most of them in early 1945: Auschwitz by the Soviets in January, two of the last ones only in April: Bergen-Belsen by the British, Dachau by the Americans. The survivors of the camps gave the Allies a horrific sight: skin-and-bones, emaciated, starving human beings, barely alive. The number of survivors is estimated to be around 200,000. The number of Jews killed by the Nazis is well above six million.

Concerning the persecution of the Jews in Hungary: after 1933, when Hitler rose to power in Germany, the right-wing government of Hungary was trying to make an alliance with the new Nazi regime, hoping that, with their help, the country could regain territories that had belonged to Hungary for centuries but had been expropriated by the 1919 Treaty of Versailles, when two-thirds of Hungary's territory was given to the countries surrounding it, territory with five million ethnic Hungarians, one-third of all Hungarians living in the Carpathian Basin. To recover these lands, Hungary slowly moved closer to Nazi Germany through the next few years. In 1938, the Munich Conference awarded Hungary a Hungarian-inhabited area in Czechoslovakia, and in 1939, 1940, and 1941, further territories were given back and annexed to Hungary. By 1941, most ethnic Hungarians lived in the enlarged territory of the Kingdom of Hungary. But the price of these regained territories, regained with Nazi-German assistance, was very high.

By 1941, the Jewish population of this enlarged territory of Hungary was about 725,000, not counting the almost 100,000 Jews who, in fear of facing persecution, became Christian but, as it turned out, were still considered racially Jews by the Nazis. About 50 percent of the Jews lived in the capital city, Budapest. The Hungarian government started to issue the first anti-Jewish laws in 1938, limiting Jewish participation in the economic and cultural life of the country. For example, in universities the so-called *numerus clausus* system was introduced, by which only a small percentage of Jews were admitted to higher education. In 1939, Hungary introduced a new draft system by which Jewish men of draft age had to join the military for forced labor. Many Jewish men died, particularly in war zones, in this so-called labor service. Although in 1941, in spite of their many restrictions, Jews lived in relative safety in Hungary. Nevertheless, terrible atrocities did already happen. During the summer months 18,000 Jews, labeled "foreign nationals," were forced to leave their homes, and were taken to German-occupied Ukraine, where most of them were murdered. In 1942 about 1,000 Jews were killed in the southern part of Hungary, in an area just regained from Yugoslavia.

Beginning in 1942, when the Germans were defeated at Stalingrad and started their long retreat—and Hungary, fighting on the eastern front, lost tens of thousands of soldiers—Miklos Horthy, the regent of Hungary, made several attempts to get out of the alliance with Germany. Germany radically stopped these attempts when, on March 19, 1944, the German army invaded Hungary, Hitler created a pro-Nazi government, and the country's German occupation began. From the beginning of this occupation, in April 1944, the situation of the Jewish population in Hungary radically changed, and their violent persecution began, called by the Nazis the "Final Solution." As elsewhere, after the restrictions, confiscations, and ghettoizing, the transport of Jews into concentration camps started. During May, June, and July of 1944, about 430,000 Hungarian Jews—and those identified by the Nazis as Jews—were taken in freight cars into death camps, most of them to Auschwitz, destined for elimination.

In October 1944, Horthy again tried to break the alliance with Nazi Germany and make peace with the Allies. The Germans prevented this step by ousting Horthy's government and giving full power to Ferenc Szálasi and his brutally anti-Semitic Arrow Cross Party. The new regime quickly started a reign of terror in the Hungarian capital. Within four months, tens of thousands of Jews were killed in Budapest, shot on the banks of the Danube River and then thrown into the river. Thousands of others were forced to walk in death marches toward Germany.

The plight of the Jews in Budapest was different from that of the rest of the country. Jewish leaders started negotiations with the SS and thus tried to save lives. They came to the conviction that the best way to save Hungarian Jews (the last Jewish community in Nazi-occupied Europe) was to negotiate with the German authorities. These Jewish leaders were able to found the Relief and Rescue Committee of Budapest to provide Jews with fake documents. They worked together with foreign diplomats such as the Swedish Raoul Wallenberg; the Swiss Carl Lutz; Angelo Rotta, apostolic nuncio of the Vatican; and others. While serving as a Swedish diplomat in Budapest between July and December 1944, Raoul Wallenberg issued thousands of protective passports and sheltered Jews in buildings designated as Swedish territory. As the senior Vatican representative in Budapest, Angelo Rotta took a lead in establishing an "International Ghetto," consisting of several dozen modern apartment buildings to which large numbers of Jews were brought—eventually 25,000—and to which the Swiss, Swedish, Portuguese, and Spanish legations, as well as the Vatican, affixed their emblems.

The Arrow Cross continued their orgy of violence, raiding even the International Ghetto and murdering Jews, as Soviet forces approached the city. During these terrible times, heroic Hungarian individuals, families, and churches were hiding thousands of Jews in their homes, a very dangerous undertaking: if the hidden Jews were found, not only those hidden but also the ones who were hiding them were executed.

Rotta and Wallenberg were among the few diplomats to remain in Budapest. Following the Soviet conquest of the city, Wallenberg was seized by the Russians and taken to Moscow, from where he was never released.

Of the 150,000 Jews who had lived in Budapest when the Germans arrived in March 1944, almost 120,000 survived to liberation—almost 100,000 in the ghettos and a further 25,000 hiding out in Christian homes and religious institutes across the city. Rotta was recognized as "Righteous Among the Nations" by Yad Vashem in 1997.

In September 1944, Soviet forces crossed the Hungarian border. The war raged in the country for many months. The entire country of Hungary was liberated from Nazi occupation by the Soviet army by April 4, 1945, only to begin a new, forty-five-year-long Soviet occupation and the rule of a Communist government. During World War II, approximately 300,000 Hungarian soldiers and more than 600,000 civilians died, including among them well over 400,000 Hungarian Jews and 28,000 Roma (gypsies), in concentration camps and death marches.

Klára Kardos

In this context of World War II, we can look at the plight of Klára Kardos, born on October 5, 1920. We read in St. Paul's Letter to the Romans, "Where sin increased, grace abounded all the more" (Rom. 5:20, RSV). Paul's statement was fully realized in her life. Her parents were Jewish, but her mother had converted to the Catholic faith before the birth of Klára, so the baby was baptized as a Catholic. Klára's parents divorced, her mother remarried, and they lived in a small village, in a rural environment. Klára received a Catholic education, along with her sister Zsuzsi, younger by ten years. From the age of twelve, Klára continued her schooling in the important provincial town of Szeged, including her university studies. She received her doctorate in 1942. She graduated also from the Ward College in Budapest and received a diploma to teach religion.

When Hungary was invaded in the spring of 1944 and occupied by Nazi Germany, and the violent persecution of the Jews started, Klára was living in Szeged far away from her family. Her family was deported from another city, Nyiregyháza, and every member of the family except Klára perished in the Holocaust. On June 6, 1944, along with other Jews, Klára was taken to the ghetto of Szeged, and after a true *via dolorosa*, on June 28, she arrived in Auschwitz. There, she was considered healthy enough for forced labor; with other prisoners, she was taken to Salzwedel in Germany, and she worked as a forced laborer in an ammunition factory.

The camp was liberated by American forces on April 14, 1945. Liberation found her in a state of total exhaustion. Her recovery took several months, after which she returned to Hungary. She never married. For a while she worked as a teacher, but because of her religious faith the Communist dictatorship fired her. From this time on, she supported herself by typing and translating. She also wrote some religious *samizdat* publications, which brought her constant harassment by the Communist police. Because of this persecution, when she found a possibility to leave the country in 1970, she moved to Austria. In Klagenfurt, Hungarian Jesuit fathers published a quarterly magazine named *Szolgálat* (Service) and published Catholic books and sent them to Hungary. Klára joined these Jesuits, and her presence, her tremendous capacity of work, her Christian faith and exceptional intellect, her erudition and familiarity with several languages, all made her indispensable in this apostolic activity. She was a true apostle, dedicating her life completely to this project, and worked literally day and night. She lived in great simplicity like a monk, and she frequently offered even her modest salary to publish a book. In the early 1980s she contracted brain cancer. After a lengthy illness, she passed away on September 25, 1984. Her remains were taken back to Hungary and buried in Budapest.

For a while she was reluctant to talk about her ordeal at the concentration camp. Years later, her friends convinced her to write down her experiences. She wrote the account in a very simple, matter-of-fact manner, an almost emotionless narration, without any sensationalism. Her *Auschwitz Journal* became a unique document, showing the suffering of double persecution of Christian Jews in the camp: first by the misery at the camp and the systematic terror of Nazi commanders, and second by the other Jews, who blamed the Christian Jews as traitors and considered them the reason for their suffering God's punishment.

At the camp, younger women were not killed, but were destined for forced labor: they were taken to German ammunition factories. The book is a very objective, almost emotionless, but a highly intelligent and observant description of the horrors of the concentration camp. Klára consciously accepted the cross as participation in the sufferings of Christ.

THE AUSCHWITZ JOURNAL

ONE
□
TOWARD
AUSCHWITZ

■ Tuesday morning, June 20, 1944

In the midst of vague rumors and preparations, the brief, now unambiguous, command explodes: we have one hour; we must all pack up what we can take along. "You can take only as much as you can carry in your hands!"

The command was not executed literally because they were taking us away by carriage. But the furniture that was crowded together in very limited spaces, a large portion of the food, supplies, and clothing . . . everything had to be left there. You can imagine the mood of this hour.

My packing was very simple indeed: just the bare minimum of the most needed items. As we were leaving, the apartments were sealed. (A ridiculous formality: I should not even need to mention that within a very short time nothing movable was left there.) And in our room was hanging on the wall—I left it there deliberately—the crucifix.

The carriages start moving. As we are carried on the open horse-drawn carts, we see around us the sobbing people of Szeged. They look at us, powerless and unable to help as we pass by.

For the time being, we are taken to the Korona Street ghetto, which we find already evacuated. Here we meet the residents of the other "white house" and it's a great joy to see again my dear classmate Kati B. and her younger sister.

Next comes the "customs examination." The female clerk assigned for this task takes away from us all of our money and anything valuable, jewelry, watches, fountain pens. One woman has a nervous breakdown. When my turn comes, the person in charge looks stunned at my wrist watch: on the face of it the picture of the Sacred Heart of Jesus is painted. She has not the heart to take away the wristwatch and my fountain pen—in a few words she interrogates me as to who I am and how I got here, then stealthily she puts the items back into my hands.

After we get through all this, we are put back on the carts in pouring rain and transported onward to the brick factory. In my lap, I'm holding a woman with heart disease.

We enter into a huge, cavernous factory hall. Upstairs on the second level, in a corner, eight of us settle down: my landlady with her daughter, Kati B. with her sister, two of the M. family, a shopgirl, and me.

■ The brick factory of Szeged, June 1944

The Jewish population of Szeged and its surroundings for a wide radius—about eleven thousand people—is crowded together here. The most awful consequence of this crowding concerns the water supply—since the only well of the factory, of course, is not in the least able to satisfy the needs of so many people. Here we get acquainted for the first time with those horrible emergency latrines that I will have the good luck to encounter later again in Auschwitz. Almost the entire day is spent by standing in line at the well, or at the kitchen. . . .

On Thursday, my returned wristwatch is lost: what the "enemy" had no heart to take, the comrades take care of. Oh, how many times will they show themselves worse than the enemy!

Here I meet the family of my aunt from Szentes, our family doctor from the same town, and more acquaintances from Szeged. The whole thing starts taking some dreamlike, unlikely character. On the one hand, we have been thrown out of our everyday environment; on the other hand, all these people from that environment are unexpectedly thrown together: this is what gives the strange impression. This will also be our dominant experience in Auschwitz at the beginning, until the cruel reality will not wash away all doubts.

We will spend a few brief days here, but this cannot be known ahead of time. Of course, we see that the present situation cannot be sustained for a long time, if not for any other reason, because of the danger of disease. A so-called census is being taken. They take records on everyone's occupation. There are rumors about a "Berlin transport" for which they are making a list. Everyone is in a terrible dilemma about whether to go or to stay. Here one cannot last very long, but there—who knows what is waiting for us.

The roll call takes place in the evening. Our hearts are throbbing in our throats. Everyone is looking for his or her name. The result is that, in general, the more influential Jews with more connections are on the list. We "proletarians" have been left out.

■ ■ ■

As it turned out later, this transport landed in Austria where, in comparison to what was waiting for us in Auschwitz, they had a wonderful life. The families were allowed to stay together, their hair was not shaved, they got into the houses of peasants where they had to do farm work but they did not suffer want in food or in anything else. When later I met a few of these Austria deportees, I almost had the impression that they were not the real deportees. But later when I read the book of Father Lenz on what they went through in Dachau, I had to feel that our experiences were nothing in comparison to theirs. There was a wide range in the quality of concentration camp life, but one thing was common everywhere: the loss of homeland and freedom.

■ ■ ■

Here our priests are unable to come after us to bring the consolation of religion, messages from our friends, and, above all, the Eucharistic Christ, although they really do try. The bishop himself comes to visit us, along with Father M. The news spreads like wildfire, and we all crowd toward the gate, but the "leadership" of the camp does not allow them to enter. They just wave to us with large green tree branches from beyond the gate.

The crowding together in the brick factory lasts from Tuesday to Saturday. During the hours of Saturday morning the command strikes us: pack up right away! It is raining inconsolably. Sitting on our bags, crowded together, we are waiting. Right after lunchtime, in the early afternoon, they make us walk, obviously hoping that at that time we will create the least stir. Indeed, maybe it is the bad weather or the scare, for the people of Szeged hide in their houses, and this time they do not wave goodbye to those who are just beginning their Calvary. This walk is dreadful! The brick factory is not too far from the Rókus railroad station, but there are among us elderly people, sick people, and children, and everybody is loaded with bags far beyond their strength. These unfortunate people are trying to save whatever is possible even now.

Had they known that everything that they were dragging along with the remainder of their strength would within three days be in the possession of total strangers, and at best would enrich the "Canadian"[1] workers in Auschwitz. . . . But we would not have thought of such a possibility even in our worst nightmares! It's true, this is the WAY! Screwed-up faces, abandoned luggage, gendarmes, a few scared passers-by on the streets. . . . It's possible that the streets were emptied by force ahead of us. As I remember, by this time I had just one small bag with me.

Then at last, at last we reach the train station where, by seventies, they jam us in the freight cars waiting for us. When the car is packed they shut the door on us

1   Canada was the nickname given by the prisoners to the front area of the Auschwitz camp, where the prisoners' luggage was sorted by other, more privileged prisoners.

and for a long minute the blackest darkness surrounds us: the mass of people crowded on top of each other. . . . Like in hell! Then they open the door just a crack to let in some air. If anyone dares to approach that crack, he finds himself looking into the barrel of a loaded weapon. In the same way, the guards tell us that nobody should dare to peek out through the small opening on the opposite wall of the car because he will be shot. They tell us also that we should remain silent, that we should behave well, and that not one of us should be missing at our arrival. For this the leader of our wagon, Laszlo R., is responsible with his life, but so are all of us as a group. If someone happens to die during the trip, we cannot throw out his body! It sounds like a bad joke, but the matter is deadly serious. Later, at the time of the winter transports, it will happen more than once that a good number of people in a railroad car arrive dead into the camps.

Seventy people in a railroad freight car are many, but what really makes the situation unbearable is the enormous amount of luggage, and in addition the pots and pans and jars of jam in great number that we have to protect with special care. . . .

And so that the nerves stretched to the breaking point will suffer even more—no one knows for what reason—there is a full twenty-four-hour period of waiting. Sunday . . . a sad Sunday indeed!

Only then comes a few minutes of relief when, using a short period of calm, Kati and her sister start to pray aloud. Following that, I recite—just from memory—a sermon of Sandor Sík on the meaning of suffering.

Sunday evening, our train is at last pulling out of the station. Goodbye, Szeged! Goodbye, precious city where we received so much material and spiritual good, so much intellectual wealth, so much love, and so much enriching suffering! Will we ever see you again? We are in God's hands! Let us trust in his infinite mercy!

■ ■ ■

One year later, in the Easter issue of the little devotional magazine *Margaret Flowers*, my good spiritual director Father Cs., recalled my "taking off" in these words, with some poetic embellishment:

K. K., the deportee of heroic spirit, left the reception camp on the feast of the Sacred Heart of Jesus with a triumphant smile on her face for the road of sufferings. With superior spirituality, she carried as the jewel of Christ's dishonor the badge[2] that was, in those times, degrading, and she wore it as bridal jewelry when partaking of Holy Communion, still able to be united with her divine Bridegroom. Since then, she disappeared without a trace. . . . Will she ever return to Szeged? Only God can say. We can only hope. But her heroic spirit that was shining from her soul showed the world that the soul, even in a body trampled underfoot, in the midst of ignominy, can be victorious over her oppressors, those people far below her dignity. One of her last words was that she wanted to atone for the sins of her people.

As I said, this image is too idealistic, but in its essence it is true. I don't have to mention that the people for whose sins I longed to atone were the Hungarian

2 This is a reference to the yellow "star of David" that the Jews were obliged to wear on their garments.

people, which does not mean that it would have been foreign to me to atone for my poor fellow companions in distress, for my race.

■ ■ ■

In any case, those three dreadful days in the freight car, from Sunday to Wednesday, are a good opportunity for atonement, but they do not leave much of the "triumphant smile."

Of course, we do not receive anything to eat, but we do not need it either. After all, we brought too much with us anyway. At least our bags grow somewhat smaller, since they are the cause of never-ending quarrel and strife. There is much trouble also with obese people. Of course, they are not at fault for their bulkiness, but in such a situation it becomes quite an antisocial thing. Somehow the two opposite walls of the freight car became "independent" of each other and there is constant bickering between them.

It is end of June, very hot days. In the overcrowded and almost completely sealed cars the heat is beyond the capacity of human endurance. We crave water, but there is barely any to be had. The only ones who come off well from all this misery are our guards, the German hyenas, because for some petty services they carry out barter transactions of great value with the desperate wagon-dwellers.

And, of course, the constant squabbling is compounded by threats from outside: if there is any noise, they will shoot. . . . When we pass a train or when we stop somewhere, the outside world is not allowed to notice that in the freight cars living, suffering men and women are crowded.

Seventy people in one car! For us this seems to be the apex of horrors—and later, when the Trans-Danubian and Budapest transports make the same trip with a hundred or a hundred-twenty jammed in a wagon?—It is difficult even to imagine it.

And those nights! In total darkness here and there flares up the flame of a match. We have to be careful that the light cannot be seen through the ventilation slit. During the first night one of the men is taken ill. Among our fellow passengers there is an insane shoemaker who, amid the screaming, mainly of the younger ones, takes walks in the wagon during the night and steps now here, now there, on people squatting and huddling in the most impossible positions.

Add to all this the constant, anguished guessing: What will tomorrow bring? Where are we going? What will happen to us? . . . The most absolutely absurd, horrifying rumors are circulating. To look out of the wagon is strictly forbidden, but somehow the news spreads that we're traveling toward the border, toward the North. . . . It's a strange thing, and in retrospect it seems even incomprehensible, but up to the very last moment we are unable to believe that, indeed, they will take us out of the country.

All in all, the immediate consequence of the random, nonsensical rumors is that people feverishly start dressing up. Whatever clothes they are able to put on from their bundle they slip on themselves: underwear, blouse, dress, coat—everything. While they are dressing, I take out from my small suitcase the few precious souvenirs I am carrying with me—my parents' telegram, their last postcard, and a few photos, among them the last picture of my younger sister with her two beautiful, long braids from the time of our sojourn in Nyiregyháza. I tear all of them to small bits and pieces and throw them out of the wagon. Then I spoon out the cranberry preserve that I received from my family a while ago, and I throw out even the little jar. They should not get into unauthorized or unworthy hands, or perhaps even sacrilegious hands, these things I consider holy. I put my rosary around my neck and wait for what will come next.

Monday afternoon: Kassa (Cosice), the border! Here they gave us a "speech" that, in essence, is: "They're taking you to work. If you behave well, you'll be well off!"

Here there is another so-called customs examination—and after some standing, the train rolls over the border. We are no longer in the territory of Hungary. The fatherland where we were supposed "to live and to die,"[3] to which we are attached with such a natural devotion, cuts us out of itself like a noxious boil.

But did they do it? And not, rather, Hitler's terror? We are passing among barren rocks covered with lime flowers. These are the sets for this bleak journey toward total uncertainty.

3   This is a line from a famous Hungarian patriotic poem, "Szózat [Anthem]" by Mihály Vörösmarty.

Does it ever come to my mind, in those minutes, the only other time that I left my country behind: as a happy and excited university student who was traveling for a study trip to Florence?

At that time, it was somewhat different. Now they're driving us like a helpless herd, and no one knows where. . . .

Even on Wednesday, June 28, in the morning of the eve of the Feast of Saints Peter and Paul, when the train comes to a halt and the doors of the freight cars are opened, we still don't know where we are. We will find out with great difficulty.

But even if we knew, it would not help much, for one could ask: How many are there among us (was there even one?) who during his or her entire life has ever heard this name, the infamous name that, since then, has become known all around the world?

We have arrived at Auschwitz!

TWO
□
BECOMING ACQUAINTED
WITH CAMP LIFE

Auschwitz, its Polish name *Oswiecim*, is located in territory that was at that time part of the "German Empire" but was in reality in northern Poland.

Among the great number of "work camps" (*Arbeitslager*), Auschwitz received a sad notoriety as the "annihilation camp" (*Vernichtungslager*).

It was here that our transport, one among so many that came from the Hungarian Plain, arrived during the morning hours of June 28, 1944.

Since then, a great many books have been written about what took place here. Documents have been published; films have been made about it. People frequently turn to me with the question: "Is everything true that is written in the books?" I must confess, I have not read even one of these "death-factory books." Am

I perhaps afraid to recall the bad memories? Not at all! I just do not consider it worth doing. Only a spiritual point of view can make such a book more than just a document or an indictment, but unfortunately, I know that I would not find this in them. Documents I do not need, and I do not want to accuse. "Not to hate: to love, just to love have I been born!" every Christian can say with Antigone.

In the "death-factory books" one can find some dreadfully dark tone and coloration, some extremely pointed stagelike dramatic character that I don't like at all.

Father Lenz expresses superbly this mistake:

In word and in picture, they're unveiling now the camps of horror. However, these can create in the "uninitiated" a psychologically wrong impression. The terrible images and confessions are true, but this was not daily camp life. And when they lasted for a longer period of time, they did not look so horrific.

(*Christus in Dachau* [*Christ in Dachau*], p. 94)

In my own way, I verbalized it in these terms: "It did not matter for me that after my death they'll make lampshades of my skin, or that they will boil soap of my bones; but when I had a cold and I did not have a handkerchief to blow my nose in: that was unpleasant." In other words: it is one thing to suffer it, and it is another thing to look at it from the outside.

But now that I have sat down to write, maybe it would have been better—this is how I was arguing within myself—to scan through a few of these books. Fourteen years have passed since then, and, I must admit, many things have dropped out of my memory, and many facts I did not know even then. But it is not such details that I want to make a record of here. And I don't flatter myself with the idea either that I'm trying to build a small, modest copy of the magnificent cathedral of Father Lenz from the point of view of a Hungarian. We did not have an overall view of countries and nations. We did not suffer such horrible things as the priests of Christ in Dachau. But we did not have a chapel either, we did not have the Eucharistic Christ, and we did not have even one priest among us. And as Christians, we were just a small island in the ocean.

All this would be too beautiful and too unequivocal in our case. But I want to write down how we tried "to remain human in the midst of inhuman circumstances," and also, how we found along the way expressions of love again and again, many times where we least expected it. And by the time I get to the end of my story, perhaps I'll be able to prove the excellent statement that, rejoicing, I read in the book quoted above:

No school in the whole world would have given me spiritually such tremendous values as this school of suffering in the camp did. All the gold and wealth of the earth would not be worth for me as much as the five camp-years.
(*Christus in Dachau*, p. 69)

This is what someone said who suffered this hell on earth for five years! It would be for me the greatest reward for this book, if I succeeded in contributing just the smallest hint that these words are true.

Of course, it would have been better to start writing sooner when the memories were more vivid. Looking at it, however, from the aspect of sifting, the longer interval did not hurt. Among so many other things to do, one gets down with some difficulty to a job that one does not consider to be of primary importance. Yet persons whose words I value highly never stopped encouraging and urging me. Only during the last few months did the events "conspire" to spur me to action. Well, let's get over with it at last! If it does some good even for one soul, it will be worth it! I considered it necessary to mention this here in advance, standing at the gate of the Auschwitz camp, so that whoever will read it will be clear about this: in width, in proportion, in being interesting, he should not expect much. But one thing will resound for the ears of those who can hear, the big leitmotif of divine Providence, "the breadth, and the height, and the depth of the love of Christ" (Eph. 3:18). Let this book be the grateful acknowledgment of this reality!

■ ■ ■

Tortured and broken after the horrible voyage, we arrive. Everybody gets off the train with all their bags. Then, all at once, the order comes: we have to leave everything there! They say that our bags would be transported after us by trucks. It does not even need to be said: we will never see any of it ever again!

In the camp there is an area reserved—separated, of course, from the rest of it—where the prisoners of a more privileged position are busy with sorting and classifying the contents of the bags. In the vocabulary of the camp language this area is called "Canada," with reference to the gold miners of that country. One can imagine how much these people "organize" for themselves! To "organize" is one of the best-known concepts of camp life. It means to obtain something in an impermissible way. I could say also: to make any sort of subsistence for oneself, since in reality, nothing is permitted.

Poor people! Poor individuals, cleaving to the earth! And yet, the despoliation of their belongings is the smaller, the much smaller part of what is waiting for us already in these first instances. That first moment, that is the most terrible among all. As we are standing at the head of the road leading into the camp, the SS soldiers shove people apart: men are separated from women; then on one side the young people, on the other side the children, the elderly, the pregnant mothers. . . . On one side, the road leads to life (oh, what kind of a life!), on the other side, to death. Of course, we do not know this yet, and even the SS men try to lighten the despair of the torn-apart families by some pious lie: "Now you're going to take a bath. It would be strange to keep men and women together. . . . Afterward you'll meet again!"—Does some feeling of compassion prompt them to say this? Or do they just want to prevent a big scene? Or has lying already become their mother tongue?—I think it is simply unpleasant for them to see our despair.

The corner of the camp of Auschwitz! How many husbands and wives, how many parents and children see each other here for the last time! It is among the greatest rarities that someone, through a set of fortunate coincidences, is able to receive news about a family member. I remember what excitement arises at the news that the husband of one of our fellow prisoners is working in the neighboring men's camp! This sudden breaking of natural family bonds is a terrible blow, and it is doubled for Jews because their family ties are especially close.

Of course, this whole operation of pushing people into various groups is carried out by sheer guesswork. That's how it could happen, for example, that the mother of the Sz. girls remains with us just because somehow she looks younger, but my house lady is put among the elderly and Kati's mother also. The four of us—Liza, Kati, Zsuzsi, and I—stay together.

■ ■ ■

How many times in my mind did I picture my loved ones on this fateful corner of the camp! The long, painful travel and the violent separation from her children probably had broken my mother so much that she must have been placed right away among the elderly. Even if my sister did not go with our mother, later on she probably signed up honestly, because also we received the summons that those below sixteen years of age must come forward because they would receive better treatment. And they were taken immediately to the crematorium. The only exceptions were the twins, because on those Mengele, the infamous principal physician of the hospital, performed experiments.

■ ■ ■

Liberated from all our baggage, we march lightly into the camp, carrying nothing but a handbag. On the way, in the hot summer sun, we see some stunted little trees, and camping under them, a strange group of people. They are waving at us with great interest. A horde with shaved heads and striped clothes—they must be gypsies! We, poor naïve people that we are, do not even have a hunch that within an hour we all will be exactly such "gypsies"!

The bath! It is a completely uncanny feeling to stand in the midst of a naked mass of flesh, in the presence of men! We have to take off our clothes and the SS guards come into the bath with us and stay among us. After our clothes, we lose something else: our hair. Since we are women, for most of us it was terribly painful to be shaved bald. And, of course, it is also unpleasant because the scorching sun hits our heads directly, and we also feel more intensely the cold of the night. In the camp, what gives one "rank" is the length of one's hair, and in this there is a reason beyond vanity, because the longer hair means a longer stay at the camp and more experience. By this people from one or another region can distinguish each other, since on those from Transylvania and Upper Hungary, who have been at the camp since spring, the "headgear" has regrown pretty well. I try to inquire after my parents and sister among those from Upper Hungary—but I do not get even the smallest news about them, although there were even among them people from Nyiregyháza.

The immediate leaders of the barracks are Slovak and Polish Jews. By this time they have suffered this hell on earth for five years, and they could hardly forgive us for only starting to live there now. They make our lives more difficult—much more than the German leaders, whom we see very seldom anyway.

After the bath comes the clothing. We receive the clothes of a different transport, without any regard for sizes, matching, or sorting—as the saying goes: "as the tree falls so it will lie." Added to them are the striped camp capes and wooden shoes. It is very hard to get used to the latter, as they pinch our bare feet. Walking is extremely painful, especially for those whose shoes do not fit—and there are quite a few such. Additionally, finding someone who will exchange them for a pair that would be less excruciating is very difficult.

When we are finished, first the camp unit is formed to which we become so much accustomed during our life out there: we have to stand in ranks of five and march in this order. This rule is sacrosanct! With our bald heads, we must look like marching boys. By the way, I am told that being without hair does not change my outward appearance much, and looking at my reflection on a windowpane, I have the same impression.

On the way, we meet with those who have been there for a long time before we arrive. They give us some bread along with some encouraging words. This means a lot for us, especially the former, since they give from what little they have—both are reassuring flashes of humaneness.

We have to line up in front of Barracks #8. Here they take our personal data. Of course, we can say whatever we want because our personal documents were left in the disinfecting chamber, and clearly they were all burned.

When finished, we enter the large hall of the barracks. It seems that this so-called Camp B3 is a new part of the huge, constantly spreading camp that is still under construction. One of the various consequences of this fact is that there is no furniture in the barracks. Of course, cabinets we do not need, as we have nothing to put in them. We do not need a table either because we can hold our bowls of food on our knees while we are eating. But the hall has neither chairs nor cots, which would help some. Thus, we have to sit on the floor with crossed legs, strictly in a row of five ranks, and we are forbidden to turn our heads, to look back, or to say a word!

All at once I hear a timid voice. Little Zsuzsi D. is trying to negotiate with her neighbor. Now I'm already unable to get to Kati's, and I must remain with my unit of five.

■ ■ ■

Aunt Eva (Eva H., a *Stubendienst* or room captain) receives us. We are entrusted first of all to her care. She is also the one who gives us the first instructions. We learn that here our daily prayer and sacrament is the *Zahl-Appel*, that is, roll call—the procedure for which I will describe later.

"Aunt Eva" is from Slovakia and, basically, she is not hard-hearted. She is a masculine-looking figure. When her cry of alarm sounds in the barracks, "For coffee!" we jump because, taking turns, we have to tote our food from the kitchen. "Aunt Eva" walks with a big stick; she even threatens us with it, to give more weight to her words. Her favorite epithet is "You cow!" She is always threatening us with the crematorium if we do not do something properly; she especially talks to us about the "cremated Czechs." We laugh at her. We cannot even believe that it is true.

■ ■ ■

I, for my part, was only able to believe it much, much later, when I already had returned home, under the weight of irrefutable facts that the crematorium was indeed in operation there, in fact, every hour of the day. I must believe it because, after all, not one elderly, not one young, not one disabled person surfaced from Auschwitz. By the way, of course, there is nothing surprising in the fact that a regime that did not know God and stood on the principle of the *Übermensch*, or "superior man," annihilated all those members of the "inferior race" whom it could use for work. After all, they are nothing more than useless mouths. The way the whole operation was performed could be even called "humane" because they told the victims that they were going to take a bath, and that was why they got into the gas chambers, where from the showerheads, instead of water, gas gushed forth so that even before they could realize what was happening, they were already dead. Then the corpses were swallowed up by the crematorium works.

So that absolutely nothing about this secret workshop could get out to the public, most of the crematorium workers themselves ended their lives there. This came to be known from those few who, as a result of some miracle, emerged from there alive.

Thus we did not take seriously the threats of Aunt Eva, just as we could not take seriously this whole situation, no matter how deadly serious it was. A dream, an unlikely confused nightmare. . . . All that was realistic about it was that it surpassed the phantasms even of the most horrible nightmares.

This exhausting first day had brought along, indeed, a lot of difficulties and novelties! After all the fuss and excitement of the day, the evening "coffee" really hit the spot! Of course, one should not think of any espresso style of coffee!

After that came the "going to bed" . . . on the bare floor, of course, since there were no cots in the barracks. Even so it was overcrowded; we had to lie on our sides, and it was extremely difficult for anyone to try to turn on the other side. . . .

■ ■ ■

■ June 29, morning of the Feast of Peter and Paul

Today the universal Church is celebrating—while we start our regular daily schedule in the concentration camp.

Morning! I should rather say dawn or night! At what hour they rouse us from sleep, we have, of course, no idea, since none of us has a watch. I know only that the stars are still shining in the sky. At this location with its rather high elevation the nights are cold, and we are very cold indeed while we are getting up and assembling. Quickly out to the "restroom"! O those terrible latrine ditches at the edge of the camp! Not even the restroom buildings are completed yet. Then lining up for the *Appel.*

It is necessary to get better acquainted with this concept, because during our stay in Auschwitz it is our main occupation. Essentially *Appel* is the taking stock of the prisoners. This is how it takes place: the population of a part of the camp, grouped by barracks, lines up in ranks of five. The barracks supervisors (*Blockälteste*) count the group, then the camp supervisor (*Lagerälteste*) walks in front of the ranks and checks the number. From time to time—and this goes along with a great stir and excitement—"the German woman," the SS woman, also comes for the purpose of control.

Zahl-Appel is held twice each day: in the morning and in the afternoon. The one in the morning starts at early dawn and lasts into the late morning. The one in the evening completes the daily program just around dusk. Normally it takes several hours of standing, but if some offense has taken place in the camp or someone for some reason is absent and the number is not complete, it is woe on us! After all, they cannot think of anything other than that someone has attempted an escape. On such occasions the *Appel* lasts as long as the missing person has not turned up, either for the whole camp or, in a more fortunate case, just for the barracks in question. The "all for one and one for all" principle comes into display in full measure. It can last up to four or even eight hours!

During the *Appel* all talking is strictly forbidden. Whoever is caught talking is clouted on the face. Naturally, if there happens to be no supervisor nearby, a few whispered words to the immediate neighbor are said. But there is no chance for a conversation.

What can we do while standing in line for hours? We can think of home, of those whom we love. We can pray. . . . And then it really is handy that, through the years, I stored in my mind with so little an effort a vast number of poems! Unfortunately, during these hours I am able to entertain only myself, but even that means so much to me.

No need to mention that while standing motionless for hours, the blazing summer sun burns our bald heads unbearably. But covering the head is strictly forbidden! If someone has obtained some rag for that purpose, either by tearing it off her underwear, or "organizing" it some other way, she has to be very careful indeed. She can only put it on her head every once in a while when there is no guard nearby, because if she is caught, they confiscate the rag immediately and, on the top of that, she is also slapped on the face.

It will be a mystery for me ever after how I am able to tolerate this at all when at home I have very little tolerance for hot weather. But there we can take many things. In general, we are in better health there than ever. For those who have a heart condition, the clean, sharp air is downright good. The new situation demands and unifies all our physical and spiritual energies so much that, so to speak, we do not have time left to worry about our usual, smaller maladies.

When the *Appel* is over, we receive a bowl of hot soup. What a heavenly delight! After the hours-long standing and shivering it tastes better than coffee with whipped cream!

Afterwards we are allowed to disperse. But the sun has just risen, the ground is cold, and sitting down on the ground would make us ill. There is nothing else to do other than keep standing in small groups in the sunny spots, here and there leaning on the wall. To return to the barracks during the day is forbidden. Well, we must look like quite the pretty "gypsy caravan."

Then, as the sun is glaring stronger and stronger and it becomes sizzling hot, there starts "the fight for the shade." Because of that there is not much in this barren area. Prompted by a happy thought, some of us dig a sand cave on the edge of the ditch, and we hide there.

At noon comes the dinner. This consists of course just of one dish, and always the same: some peculiar, thickly mixed soup, with a characteristic grayish-green color and a strange taste and smell. Not everyone is able to push it down. I consume it from the first minute on in great quantities; exactly because of its negative qualities one can get abundant seconds from another prisoner or from those who mete it out. There are some who even lick the pot. This is very lucky for us—if we become weak already by that time, many of us will not be alive later! The peculiar taste of this thick soup is not only the result of the ingredients: they also put tranquilizers, bromides, in the food.

Following the afternoon *Appel* comes supper: black coffee and the daily bread-portion that one can consume easily at one sitting. It can be maybe six or eight ounces, with a little margarine, preserves, or some sausage of a sort on top.

After supper: "going to bed." Going to bed does not go smoothly. First, there are fewer blankets than people when in the cold of the night everyone could use one. "Private property" does not exist—it is everyone for oneself! It seems to me that we were to receive even our striped camp cape only later, in the fall.

Second, the space is insufficient. The less aggressive ones are squeezed out from the big hall into the hallway, which, after all, is not bad because the character of the space requires some order in lying down. While in the big hall people are lying pell-mell, in the hallway by contrast everybody is lying on the two sides, along the walls, facing each other.

At night, there is complete darkness. It is not uncommon that—considering the possibility of catching a chill from the cold—someone has to get up during the night and go to the latrine. There is among us an unfortunate woman who has kidney cramps during the night. . . .

■ ■ ■

The reader must have noticed that washing was missing from our morning routine. Yes, water! Again, this was the greatest misery! In the camp under construction, there simply was not a water system yet. Water was delivered each day in huge barrels for the kitchen. Dying with thirst, with dry tongues, forming small groups, we eyed it from a distance. The bravest ones attempted sometimes to get closer and steal some in a small container. But this was a very risky enterprise because here the guards had to apply the strongest methods: they protected the kitchen supplies with whips, and the whip was not just an ornament but was used regularly! The other possibility to "organize" water was the sewer canal. Of course, this sticky water was absolutely not potable, and even for washing it was barely usable. It was a terribly troublesome problem for us to keep ourselves and our clothing clean, even partially.

I remember on one occasion someone managed to "organize" not just a small but a larger pan of water, though it's also possible that we "purchased" it by the camp's only currency: we gave bread for it, and three of us, one after the other, wonderfully wash ourselves!

Then it was an Auschwitz specialty: the secondhand washing. When the happy owner finished her laundry, they wheedled from her the leftover water, and it went from one person to the next until the water became completely black or was completely used up.

■ ■ ■

The first thunderstorm, for which during the hot summer days we do not have to wait very long, proves that our barracks do not offer us any protection against rain. The water from the sky just pours into our room. It is at this time that we discover the best way to dry out wet clothes is body heat. There is no other choice since we do not have a spare set of clothes. At home, such an enterprise probably would result in pneumonia, yet here none of us gets sick, and we are even laughing at the situation.

But we are not in the mood of laughing during the extended night rains. It is impossible to lie down, as the water is pouring down on us. We have to get up and make a choice in a difficult dilemma: we can either get drenched by the rain and wait in this condition to be shivering in the frigid morning, or, using our blankets, try to make a tent, and accept the fact that our covers will be useless for days.

I remember well such a night: into our dark, cold barracks the rainwater is pouring. The three of us, the Katas and I, stand on the water-covered floor, hold the blanket above our heads, and to the rhythm of the monotonous "knocking" of the raindrops, counting on our fingers, we recite the Rosary with the sorrowful mysteries. From time to time a voice sounds from the outer darkness: "Are you praying? . . . May I also join in? . . ." And the prayer, strengthened by one more voice, continues: ". . . blessed is the fruit of thy womb, Jesus, who sweat blood for us . . . who carried the heavy cross for us. . . ."

For a person of culture, it is an unquenchable requirement to divide into small segments and thus keep track of the passage of time. Just let us remember the daily notch marks of Robinson Crusoe on the uninhabited island! In our case, it is important also because the passage of time—according to our strong conviction—must bring closer the end of the war and—with that—our liberation. In our barracks, I become the "calendar" from whom everyone can get information on what day of the month and of the week it is. Fortunately, I also remember the feast days of the major saints.

On a certain First Friday, a little girl starts to cry: at home she had been doing the Great Novena. . . .[4]

■ ■ ■

The first Sunday in Auschwitz. . . . The B's and the Sz's and a few more Christians gather in a small group during the morning hours.

What on earth could have prompted me when I was in the seventh grade that during art classes (since I was excused from them) I would memorize the Latin text of the ordinary parts of the Mass? I must believe that it was the foresight of Divine Providence. Our Missals are obviously torn up and burned, there is no trace anywhere of a priest, but I am able to sound the eternal word: "*Introibo ad altare Dei*. . . . I will go up to the altar of God." Of course, I have to improvise the proper parts, such as, "Let us pray. God, who allowed us to

4   The Great Novena is a Catholic devotional practice of receiving Holy Communion on the First Fridays of nine consecutive months.

celebrate these holy mysteries, grant, we beseech you, that we may praise you by our lives and our sufferings, and protect us always with your all-powerful strength. We ask this through Jesus Christ, our Lord. Amen."

We even have a sermon: at the end of the service poems are recited, the best religious poems of the Hungarian literature, from Balassi and Berzsenyi up to our days. That's the way the Christian community of Auschwitz celebrates the Lord's Day. . . .

■ ■ ■

From time to time (if I remember correctly, biweekly) they take us to the "disinfecting" building. On such occasions, we get a shower and a change of clothes. This takes place outside the camp since inside no proper structure is available for such purpose. This is a huge event for which we all prepare with great excitement fit for the occasion, and not only we the prisoners but also the leadership. We are thoroughly instructed in how we must behave.

We take off quite early, lined up in the usual five ranks, surrounded thickly with SS soldiers and bloodhounds to prevent a possible escape. It would be very difficult anyway in the completely unfamiliar area.

■ ■ ■

We leave behind the barbed-wire fences and walk through the forest. The railroad station is also on our way—real rails, real trains! We gaze astonished at these fabulous messages of the real "life" so distant from us. Then we march into Birkenau. We stand in formation in a large cobblestone courtyard, separated in groups by barracks. There is a well in the middle.

When our turn comes, we file into the bath, where we get the shower and "disinfection." The latter consists of being lightly sprayed on the hairy parts of our bodies with some disinfecting liquid. The SS are afraid of lice in their own, well-understood interest, since these insects spread the terrible typhus fever.

After that we receive "new skin" from the camp's wardrobe, simply the clothes taken off by members of some other transport. I have to add here that the clothes, including the underwear, are only disinfected but not washed! What the results of this are on women's clothes, it is better to leave to one's imagination! At times we almost die of nausea. Yet, to wash something "at home" (in our barracks)—for that, as we have seen, one needs great courage and an even greater cunning and ingenuity. And if a button falls off or the string of one's pants gets broken. . . . After all, we have nothing, absolutely nothing! Maybe you can beg for a needle and a little thread from the room captain.

Soap we purchase with bread, if we are lucky and skillful enough. Such "owners" are the subjects of general envy, and they have to protect their wealth with meticulous care: they wrap it in a little piece of rag or in a little self-made bag and wear it on their waist day and night along with their tin bowl and spoon.

When we finish, we march out in the same courtyard and wait until all the other barracks are done. Then we start our march back "home." It may happen that the clothes are fewer than the people. On such occasions the last of the barracks gets off the worst. One time I go home just in a blouse and a skirt because the underwear runs out. There is even a fellow prisoner who has to march wrapped in a blanket because of a shortage of outerwear; only the next day do they find some clothes for her.

This disinfection is dangerous for our "organized" items also. (I can no longer remember where we hid these things, whether on each other or in the barracks.) In one of the religious orders the rule is that nothing may be taken from one room into another. Well, in Auschwitz, this radical despoilment is implemented thoroughly. For small items, there are two solutions: our shoes, because they are not changed, or our mouths. This is how I am able to keep my little monogram of Christ safe. It is not without danger, even in the physical sense.

And through all these we are still alive. That dreamlike quality that characterizes our life from the beginning onward shrouds our whole existence. It is impossible to believe what is happening to us; the brain knows that it is true, but the senses simply refuse to relay the feel of reality. Thus, the general mood cannot be called particularly bad. The bromide is certainly responsible in part and also, in general, we are from the younger generation, and the whole thing has to be considered as some kind of a strange changeover. The stubbornness of the life instinct triumphs over despondency. We want to live and be alert and attentive even here! And beyond all, for those who are believers, there is the power of religion, there is the trust in Providence. There is no priest, there is no church, there is no possibility for any practice of religion, but God is in us since in him "we live and move and have our being." Here one can live out fully this wonderful reality and truth.

Slowly, I start to work out my spiritual life within the new framework of existence. I introduce the "walking meditation," immediately following the *Appels*, partly because it is cold, partly because in this way it is easier to go apart from the rest. In the tense, shivering atmosphere of the *Appel* one cannot really focus on deeper thoughts. For example, as the topic of one series of meditations, I take the text of the Holy Mass. Of course, there is no way to write down the fruits of these hours. Even the smallest piece of a pencil or a bit of scratch paper is an unreachable dream for us, and, on top of it, it is the object of the most relentless persecution from the part of our leaders. How much pain does this cause! Never a note, never a letter to loved ones.

In the absence of "real" Holy Communion, spiritual communion becomes my daily bread. There opens a wide opportunity also for "pastoral" apostolic activity. Sitting on the edge of the ditch, there are deep, spiritual counseling sessions among the camp dwellers. We also recite poems. I remember, I have to recite for Kata again and again the poem of Sándor Sík, "Bonfire Smoke." Its words echo in us with a shocking actualization as an all-encompassing program![5]

"From you they are begging for living dew!" What a beautiful, what a majestic task it is to give spirit to those who are looking for spirit: spirit from the Spirit! Dear Kata, my dear good friend! Her large, faith-filled eyes: how they drink in the word! How beneficially her quiet, confident personality affects me!

■ ■ ■

We could not stay together much longer. I met her again after my return to home. She had lost her younger sister just a few hours before liberation. They got into one of those "death marches" when the Germans would

5   At this point Klára inserts a rather long section of an even longer poem from the Catholic priest-poet Sándor Sík, who was also of Jewish background. During the 1960s Sandor Sík was the provincial superior of his religious order, the Piarist Fathers, while his twin brother, Endre Sík, was the minister of foreign affairs of the Hungarian Communist government. After the long quote Klára continues her writing by repeating a phrase from the poem.

force the starving, living-dead camp dwellers to walk from one place to another. Zsuzsi could not bear it any longer; she lay down on the roadside. Kata lay down next to her with the intention of dying with her, but the guards, by striking her with whips, forced her to get up. She had to continue to walk. By the time the American troops made it to her sister, she was probably already dead. At the least Kata never did receive any news about her. She also lost her mother. She remained here alone, all by herself. Soon she got married. Her confidential revelation was very characteristic: "I did not want to spend another Christmas alone." Later she and her husband emigrated. Currently she lives in Switzerland as a happy wife and mother.

■ ■ ■

There is even "cultural life" in Auschwitz. This takes place especially during times of the so-called barracks lockdown (*Blockspärre*), which means that for some reason nobody is allowed to leave the barracks. At such times, we settle down on the floor and hold conversations, "entertaining" each other. There is among us an opera "diva," and from time to time she is willing to delight us with her voice. Afterward comes the reciting of poems, dancing. . . .

On the 9th of July, on the birthday of my dear mother, I set up a "concert" in her honor, with the only means I have: my voice. Parts of her favorite opera, *La Traviata,* then Gounod's *Ave Maria,* and the "Christmas Lullaby" that she loved so much: "I prefer the heavenly silence. . . ." I think at that time that she is far away, yet most likely she is already very close, listening to me. . . .

I am trying to get acquainted with my fellow prisoners' moods and attitudes, first of all with those of the "real" Jews. Personally, I cannot complain: I don't remember experiencing any adverse criticism for being Christian. Of course, the basic view is present that causes a splinter in us converts' very existence. "We got put here because of you!" they say, because we abandoned Yahweh and, as a result, he took revenge on the Jewish people. Poor people! My familiarity with the Old Testament helped me a lot.

■ ■ ■

In the eyes of the Germans we, Jewish prisoners, were probably considered as some kind of exotic animal. It's strange to write this down, but filled with Nazi conceitedness and imbued with a lot of demagogic indoctrination, it did not even occur to them that we too were human beings. At the most, maybe, we were human "stuff" of which they had to give an account.

As we have seen, they were guarding this "stuff" with great care. The fence surrounding the camp was not just common barbed wire but had electric current running through it, with guard towers besides, machine guns. . . . The atmosphere was constantly heated by nervousness. For their part: maybe they'll escape; from our side: to go, just to go. No, not to try to escape. That would have been madness. But we knew that Auschwitz was only a huge reception camp from which they'll take us to work. That was what we eagerly awaited. Work is always better than nerve-wracking idleness.

■ ■ ■

And then comes July 14, Friday. Assembly, selection. The news gets around instantly: they're forming a transport. They need one hundred people. A strange disposition of Providence: I am the hundredth person. Kati and Zsuzsi are standing just behind me; they are left behind. It's possible (I don't remember exactly) that one of them can get among the one hundred but, of course, they do not want to be separated, and to switch with someone one can only go "backward."

Thus the time comes for me to say goodbye to Camp B3.

I'll never forget this uplifting moment. Oh, here you don't have to pack, to move with one's possessions, to carry luggage! How many times since then will I wish for the return of that happy state! One does not have to say goodbye to a weeping family! In the one skirt and blouse that, at that time, is all I could call my property, a short farewell to those who remain there, and "Here am I, Lord, I am at your disposal!"

In the light of the setting sun, the little band takes off.

In this mountainous area the sunsets are majestically beautiful, and we have even more opportunity to admire the sunrise: during the bone-chilling *Appel* they present us with the consolation of a truly "divine comedy."

Where to? Which way?
You know it, Lord! Whatever you want is good!

Remain in silence when God is calling;
He's summoning gently like the voice of a
    shepherd's pipe.
Get up and take off obediently,
gladly like a little dog, quietly like a lamb.

The loud man does not create anything valuable;
silence is stronger than violence.
If what you get is a belt of nails or the crimson
    flames of a spire,
just smile and say, "Our Father."

And if the voice took you on the top of the bloody
    Mountain
where the world's sins are taken away,
step meekly in front of those who'll nail you:
the shearing ranch-hand also belongs to the
    Shepherd.

(Selections from the poem of Sándor Sík, "Remain in Silence")

THREE

□

WAITING AND THE HOSPITAL BARRACKS

What can the person know about travelling, who's shivering and shaking on the shore and does not dare to throw himself into the torrent, or is struggling on the edge of the stream to get out of the current?

What can the person know about God's will, about the marvels of His love manifesting itself also in suffering, whose attention is tied to one goal: to get away, to flee from the stream of divine Providence?

Can a person talk about a road that he did not tread? About the trail on which he never climbed?

Can anyone say that there is only annihilation and death in a country in which he never wandered about?

Even the martyrs were trembling in front of their executioners, even Christ cried out in pain on the Cross. But it is also true that countless weak, fragile, and sinful persons lived and are alive on earth today who, after they walked through the path of suffering, knelt down and gave thanks to God for it. And they were guarding and carrying along with them to the tomb and even beyond that the memories of the years and days that they had spent in trials as the greatest treasure of their lives.

Let's not try to conclude to God's goodness or "cruelty" from the existence of suffering; rather let's look at our suffering and that of others in the light of God's mercy! God is infinitely wise and good. If He tolerates or even sends us suffering, it must have a divine, eternal meaning and purpose, even if we are unable to exhaust its depths. We can surmise this or that about suffering, but to understand it in its total depth is impossible.

One thing is certain: in suffering a person is able to rise out of himself to the highest level if he wants to encounter God's unfathomable mysteries face to face, "to see him with his own eyes." What God wants is not a multitude of words, not an explanation, but this encounter. And who can tell what it means to meet God in suffering? It's possible to talk about it but to express it adequately is impossible. Only the person who lived through it can understand it!

(Ferenc Sinkó, "Little Way," *Vigilia* [a Hungarian Catholic monthly], October 1958)

Our way led us toward Camp B2, also called the "Czech Camp." Here we were welcomed with great novelties. The barracks were much sturdier structures with waterproof roofs. The barracks in which our "detachment" was accommodated, and in which altogether five hundred persons slept, used to be a stable for horses, as was evident from the many metal rings on the walls. But now they were densely furnished with real cots in three-story bunks. On each of these bunks ten or eleven persons were jammed together. Due to the crowded space and the one common blanket that all people on one bunk shared, everybody had to lie facing the same direction and, if anyone had had enough of that, everybody had to turn to the other side. Although the four people in the middle were safe, those on both edges complained frequently about sleeping without a blanket.

I remained close to some of those with whom I shared the same bunk. Even after we returned to Szeged we kept in touch for a while, until we got scattered one here, one there.

Here in this camp there came into existence the alliance of Franci P., Gizi E., Éva G., and myself. I insert here the remark that, among ourselves in the camp, we addressed each other in the "German way," that is, as with married women, first the husband's family name and then the first name.

Let me stop here for a moment. A friendship (and so few bonds between a person and another person truly deserve this name) is always something solemn and great. But it was an ever-greater reality when on the whole earth we did not have anything except each other! Unfortunately, even in such circumstances, the principle of "everyone against everyone" prevailed. This was true, most of all, among the "real" (i.e., non-Christian) Jews, and I count among them also those on whom Christianity was only an external varnish.

Here and there one could see some camaraderie, but real friendships were few. This was the reason our friendship with Franci was such a great treasure. We "discovered" each other here at the B2 camp, and our friendship remained unbreakable through the difficult months all the way to the evening of liberation. Of course, this could also have happened in Szeged, where she finished at the Akademy and the Apponyi College just a few years ahead of me. It could have happened at 11 Kelemen Street since she was placed into the same house [as I was] in the "white ghetto." We could have met in the brick factory or when we were loaded into the freight cars, even in the B3 camp, after all she had trodden the same path that I did. Her husband was an inmate at a forced labor camp, but, after a short while, he escaped from there and came back to Szeged, where, looking for traces of his wife, he miraculously found his diploma abandoned at the ghetto headquarters. Franci already had a hunch at that time that for our future career we would not need a higher education. Of course, she did not know anything of her husband. At that time, they were just recently married, still without children, and she suffered deadly worries for him.

Thus, it was designed that the two of us would find each other in the B2 camp and become for each other help and a source of strength up to the end. In the "foursome alliance" the two of us got the intellectual and spiritual leadership roles. The two other women were younger, the roundish Gizi B. who was (at least at the beginning) blessed with a fortunate calmness, and the tall and skinny Éva G., whose mood was fluctuating, with an inclination toward pessimism.

In this camp, there was even water. The *Waschraum* was a separate barracks. The water flowed from two faucets on both sides into a tin trough. Here one could wash more frequently, but the biweekly disinfection continued. There was also a restroom building but the cleaning crew (consisting of men), could enter any time without any inhibition, and they commented with very unambiguous hints on what they saw.

Thus there was water, but drinking was strictly forbidden from the very beginning on. They said that the water was polluted with typhoid fever bacteria. Whether it was true or just malicious ill-will made them say it, I never found out. But it's a fact that we were very much afraid of typhoid fever, and so the morning soup and the evening black coffee represented for us all the drinkable liquid that those who had been picked to go with the SS commandoes carried to us from the kitchen with great difficulty. I got so out of habit of drinking water that even to this day I rarely do it.

■ ■ ■

As a matter of fact, we got into the Czech Camp for the purpose of quarantine, for a time of observation before they'd take us to work, to find out whether there was anybody among us contaminated with some contagious disease. This time of tests took eight days. During that, of course, our usual pattern of life continued, including that of standing for *Appel*. If it was raining—and it rained quite a lot—the *Appel* lasted even longer. Besides that task, we kept the barracks and their surroundings clean. And so that we'd do some exercise, as a preparation for work, we had to walk daily (if I remember correctly) in a circle for about one hour while holding two bricks in our hands.

Against the rain, during the day, we tried to protect ourselves with some shrewdness. We took off our underwear and hid them in our "beds"; then when we returned all wet to the barracks, we put on our dry underwear, and covered ourselves with blankets while our outerwear were spread out for drying. When the supervisors discovered this, they started to make "bed visits," and any underwear they found there were taken away.

■ ■ ■

Of the leadership of that camp I remember nothing any longer. From the room of the barracks supervisor, there frequently wafted a delicious aroma of garlic: they were cooking meatloaf for themselves by using meat stolen from our sausage rations and margarine stolen from our tiny bread ration.

Yes, it was like this up to the very end. When later, during our time of factory labor, the margarine or preserves between the two pieces of bread showed itself only in a paper-thin layer, we could be sure that we could thank our "brethren" who snuck into the kitchen. Can one use words strong enough for those unfortunate people who, in cold blood, were skimming from the rations of their comrades and fellow Jews, from rations so meager that they were barely enough for survival, so that they could have excess food? They were not just eating it: they were saving the preserves and margarine by the kilo, and also underwear and clothing—they were even buying jewelry for themselves.

The result of hunger, of the constant starvation, had already started to show itself in our company. On the one hand, as I said earlier, not everybody was able to consume the "Auschwitz porridge"; on the other hand, we painfully experienced most of all the scantiness of bread. In general, this kind of nutrition was nothing like the usual middle-class nourishment to which we were accustomed. No wonder then that the camp dwellers, during their free time, could talk for hours and hours about food and recipes. The most frequently heard lament among us was, "If I could only cook a good paprika potato again!" It was a rather modest wish!

But as for me, this kind of occupation was annoying. I did not have enough understanding for these kinds of material needs—I could say, for the human nature—of the human body, as I still frequently don't up to the present. I was born with a rather "flexible" stomach, as it turned out, and, although by "the end of times" I grew ethereally emaciated, I wouldn't dare to say that I was seriously starving at any time during my camp life. But then the good God made me blush for shame because a delayed reaction came after my return home to Szeged: no amount I ate was enough, that is, no amount I could have eaten, if, in the world after the war, during inflation, there had been enough food. At that time, this kind of fantasizing already moved my imagination also. By the way, Fr. Lenz mentions [in his book] that also among the men, even among priests, it was a general phenomenon to daydream about food items and passing on recipes. And I, on such occasions, went angrily farther away and buried myself in reciting poems in my mind. The spirit, not the body, should enforce its rights!

Another thing in which I did not participate was the spiritualistic gatherings, when by "walking" buttons and by other means they conjured the ghosts to inquire from them their own destinies, those of their loved ones, and naturally the avidly expected hour of liberation. This brought a little variety into their lives and excited their nerves, which were already overwrought anyway.

Woe to those poor persons in whom no prayer was born in the hopelessness and meaninglessness of camp-life! There is simply no other means to endure such earthly misery with true human dignity than to cling, filled with faith, to God's fatherly hands.

—FR. LENZ

■ ■ ■

It was a small thing, but for me a very painful small thing: the loss of my eyeglasses, which, in fact, may have already happened in Camp B3. In the evening, I always put them carefully in my shoes, yet, one night, someone stepped on them regardless. The glasses broke. At first I missed them very much. Later on I got used to this also; my first photo after the camp (of which I'll tell more) shows me still to be that way.

■ ■ ■

In our neighborhood was the site of Camp C, the men's camp. Of course, it was strictly forbidden to approach its boundaries. Yet we could see how, every morning, they were gathering up and carrying away, pile after pile, the dead bodies that had shriveled into dry mummies. Men survived camp life in much smaller numbers than we women. One way or another we were more tenacious and resistant, primarily, obviously, because of temperamental, spiritual reasons. The woman, created for motherhood, is trained early in life for suffering while the man is impatient. Rebellious even among normal circumstances, he can barely tolerate the physical suffering or emotional humiliation. Beyond that, the meager amount of nourishment, on which we women were somehow able to survive, was fatally inadequate for men.

One way or another, one of the barracks supervisors over in Camp C learned that his wife was among us. One day he joined the attendants of the restroom cleaners, and as such he was able to come over to us and meet her. They repeated such encounters several times, but on one occasion the SS soldiers caught them conversing with each other. They ruthlessly beat up K., but he did not even open his mouth lest his wife should hear him.

■ ■ ■

There were also pregnant women among us. Of course, these were only such women whose pregnancy was not visible at the initial "sorting out." One of these women vowed that if she had to give birth to her child she'd run against the high-voltage fence. (This was the usual, easy way of suicide.)

Another of our companions, her name was Teri, indeed gave birth to her child here. The Germans told her that the child was stillborn. In reality, they drowned the baby in a bucket of cold water and then wrapped it in old newspaper. Such a "surplus" was really not desirable to the Germans.

The sick also belonged among the unneeded "surplus." One day we had seen the inmates of a vacated hospital barracks in white nightgowns, marching in a pitiful column, obviously toward the crematorium.

■ ■ ■

So we were being prepared for work. But to be able to pass through the gate of the Auschwitz camp, a tattoo was an indispensable prerequisite. Whoever received this indelible mark was already provided with the personal identification of the inmates of the concentration camp and, beyond that, with an assurance against escape. The whole operation itself took place swiftly and without pain. With a slightly curved, sharply pointed little tool ending like a beak, they pricked or dotted with practiced swiftness the camp's initial and our number on our left lower arm. It gave us a light burning sensation, and then it was all over.

A/1248—this is what I would be from then on.

Many of us already vowed at that time that when they got home, they would have the tattoo removed. It could be done with plastic surgery. I've seen such persons: after the removal, a traitorous scar remains on the arm, which ultimately is just as telling for expert eyes as the tattoo itself. I could not understand why it is good for one to try to make the traces of one's past disappear. "It's on the right place"; that is what I used to say and what I'm still saying today. The only unpleasant consequence is that it may happen that certain strangers, after staring at it conspicuously, make some compassionate remarks—or unveil themselves as fellow sufferers. On such occasions, it is difficult to answer without making a fool of oneself. Never can I do it according to my heart's desire.

■ ■ ■

Our intellectual and spiritual life continued without interruption. We observed the Sunday "Masses" together, and on the weekdays, I observed them in my mind during the *Appel*.

I got acquainted here with two nieces from Marosvásárhely, the Király girls Ili and Ella. They were intelligent, well-educated girls who, on top of everything, could whistle perfectly in two voices. Not just anything, but opera arias and Beethoven symphonies! We could thank them for many beautiful minutes in our barracks.

But my most beautiful and most unforgettable memory from this period was completely personal. It was a rainy afternoon. I was cowering on my bunk, miraculously by myself, with my face buried in my hands. As it turned out later, my companions believed that I was grieving and weeping. Yet in this period of maybe half an hour I experienced something wonderful.

I was thinking of home, of all the persons, one after the other, whom I loved, who were close to my heart, with whom the Spirit bound me together through and in spite of all distances. As I was thinking of them, they appeared to me—I should say: they visited me or I visited them—in a much more tangible and purer closeness than I could have ever encountered them in their physical reality. I never experienced so strongly how unimportant is distance or physical separation when the spirit alone is what really counts.

■ ■ ■

We awaited, anxiously and excitedly, the end of the quarantine and our departure to work. God disposed differently; instead of the eagerly expected departure, a little-expected guest arrived: scarlet fever. The first case showed up within the previously planned eight days and then, one after the other, all the rest. We were depressed, and our leaders were mad because the quarantine had to be extended. The eight days became two months! I myself who, up to that time, also had not caught this children's disease, was among the last ones to get the infection. On one of those exact days our superiors announced, "If any other person catches the scarlet fever, she will go to the hospital . . . !"

Miraculously, Franci did not get the fever from me, although we stood next to each other and ate from the same bowl.

The course of the illness in general was quite light; there were no fatalities at all. But my scarlet fever gave me the opportunity to be able to "conduct the experiment" on a new terrain of camp life: the hospital. Since the beginning, I was almost preparing myself for it all the more because I wanted to see, experience, live through as much as possible.

■ ■ ■

The hospital barracks! My quarters for six weeks! It was a true rest and holiday for me. After the first few days my fever quickly dropped and, I can say, I spent the remaining weeks in good health. Each of us had a separate bed, which in itself was something very luxurious. Only when the sick became too many did two persons have to share one place—against which, of course, everyone protested. But even then we could still lie on our backs, not "edgeways," on our sides as in the barracks.

Here our duty was to lie in bed, which, after the extensive standing, we enjoyed very much indeed. It was also our constant duty to keep the beds in good, military order. The meals were, of course, in general the same as outside but perhaps somewhat more abundant. I remember that, by some kind of mystery, once in a while we even baked a potato on the embers of our stove. . . .

Unfortunately, I no longer remember the hospital barracks supervisor. We had more contact with the head nurse, Magda—or should have. She was not very concerned about us—but rather about her son who was living in Camp C6. Because of her privileged status, she was able to stay in contact with him. She embezzled the medicines that she supposed to distribute among us and exchanged them for cigarettes that she then gave to her son. Medical ethics in Auschwitz! Because, after all, she was supposed to be our doctor, too.

Otherwise we belonged to the notorious head physician, Mengele. This is such a name that it cannot be absent from any book about Auschwitz. From time to time—not very frequently—he showed up for visits that consisted of his going through among the beds and listening to the reports. As I remember, he asked us also, just so, how are we doing in general, and we answered fervently, "Very well!" Nobody was in the mood to say she was not doing well and in this way get a closer acquaintance with the dreaded potentate. Not much good would have resulted from that. Even these visits did not give us much joy because they were preceded by a great excitement not so much on our part but on the part of our leadership. Everything had to shine sparkling clean, and on the beds the bedding and the patients lie neatly in order, with no wrinkles on the blankets. . . .

On such days, the morning "visitations" (patients visiting each other in each other's beds) had to be cancelled. We just lay in our beds bored, until around noon "his highness" showed up. Otherwise, Mengele had a passion that already at that time was well known: the twins, as I mentioned earlier.

■ ■ ■

While I was resting at the hospital, three good friends of mine slipped from time to time under my window and (if they came in a lucky moment) they waved to me or "conducted conversation" if we were able to. In earlier times, in spite of the strict prohibition, a few bold ones had crept stealthily inside the hospital, but during the scarlet fever period (or at least while I was there) I don't remember it happening.

I made here, of course, some new acquaintances as well. I got acquainted with little Livia K., who was also a Christian. Since then she has got married and lives in Szeged even now.

Then there was Györgyi R., a woman from Budapest, whose religion, if I remember correctly, was Protestant. But she was a great devotee of St. Anthony, even to the point of superstition. I was sorry for her confusion because she had a lot of goodwill and a great heart. We chatted through long evenings, whispering at the ever-smoldering embers in the dark hospital barracks. From time to time, in the heat of discussion, we did not notice that we had raised our voices until the sick wishing to sleep shouted angrily at us. After that we whispered even more softly. Poor Györgyi! She was attached to me; she clung to me for some steadfastness. She recovered there—but only to leave us very soon. We'll hear more about her.

One day, from the bunk above mine, I heard painful whining and wailing. The little Magda G., a small woman from Transylvania, lay there. The scarlet fever affected her ear, and she got an inflammation of the middle ear. It is commonly known that this is very painful and comes with high fever. I tried to comfort her and be as helpful as I could. Meanwhile we became close friends.

Magda came from the birth village of the Hungarian poet Endre Ady and later lived at Nagyvárad (Oradea) with her husband. Soon I had the feeling that I had got into the hospital in order to meet her. The topic of our conversations quickly became the Lord Jesus, the Lord Jesus toward whom she groped with her well-meaning readiness and thirsty longing.

After we had many long talks about him, one day—maybe on the Sunday following our release from the hospital—we were walking up and down on the camp street when almost without any explanation I recited to her the entire text of the Holy Mass. She seemed to inhale the words in hushed silence and all at once, though she herself could not say why, her eyes were flooded with tears. . . .

How beautiful this is! How very beautiful this is! At that time, it was already her strong resolution, if God would help her to get home, to ask for baptism. But the baptism of desire bound her already at that time indissolubly to him for whose knowledge, by the inscrutable designs of Providence, she had to come to the camp of the Jews. Of course, these things were not completely unknown to her even before, but it was here that the work of grace unfolded in her.

In Belsen, after a short while, our paths separated. I never met Magda G. ever again but I made inquiries about her unflaggingly because I very much wished to know what happened to her, and especially whether she fulfilled her firm intention. At long last, the search ended with success. I learned that she came home, found her husband, and indeed became a member of holy mother Church. Afterwards they emigrated, and presently they live happily somewhere in Scandinavia. Thanks be to God!

One day, from the bed above mine came the sound of weeping and wailing obviously caused by pain. The little Magda G., the Jewish woman from Transylvania, was lying there.[6] The scarlet fever caused infection in her ear, and she caught inflammation of the middle ear (*otitis media*), which, as a matter of common knowledge, is very painful and is accompanied by high fever. I tried to comfort her and be helpful as much as I was able. Meanwhile we became close friends. When she got better we spent large parts of the day cuddled together, immersed in conversation. There was in her a great amount of intelligence and even more heartfelt goodwill. In spite of her being Jewish, I shared with her my secret and showed her my small monogram of Christ[7] shining silvery, and she stared at it with wide open eyes and spontaneous devotion. Yes, in the hospital this monogram was still with me. . . . On how many evenings turning into night, when my companions were already asleep, I took it in my hands and was looking at it in the gentle light of the moon shining through the window

6   The author mentioned the same Magda G. just a few paragraphs previously, but apparently forgot and so reintroduced her in this section.
7   A combination of the Greek characters Chi and Rho, XP, the letter X intersecting P at the center.

or on stormy nights in flashes of lightning! Meek Jesus! Triumphant Jesus! Perhaps on such occasions was it the most majestic: the deep darkness and intermittently the Only One triumphantly shining forth. This seemed to be exactly the reason for the storm, that we might see it all the more clearly!

> The storm and the lightning served only one purpose,
> So that my sleepy eyelashes might flicker
> So that I'd learn to see with watchfulness. . . .
>
> —SÁNDOR SÍK, "You are the good. . . ."

The militant Church. . . . The triumphant Church. . . . I kissed the little monogram. It was like a spiritual communion. My daily "Mass" took place each morning lying on the hospital's straw bed, in silent solitude. . . .

This week also passed. In the bath building there were two big concrete tubs, one of them reserved for those with scarlet fever, so that they could take a bath before returning to their own barracks. Obviously, my turn at this "ceremony" also came. The longing after cleanliness was so strong that the healthy "outsiders" also took baths in this tub frequently, not worrying about infection or contamination. . . .

Since I was among the last ones to get into the hospital, I was also among the last ones to get out from there. My three dear companions welcomed me with great rejoicing.

■ ■ ■

In the middle of September, at last, we said good-bye to Camp B2. We spent one night in Camp A, where the barracks were still built of adobe, teeming with a host of rats and mice.

In the morning, we continued our way toward the bathhouse, out of the camp. Franci and Éva—one way or another—obtained a can of apricot preserve and now, thinking "who knows where we're going, maybe we'll end up in the crematorium," they ate, or more precisely licked, the contents of the can.

The pessimism was exaggerated, because what seemed almost impossible in fact happened: we left Auschwitz, the place from which so many only left tortured nearly to death or crippled—and even more did not ever come out alive. We were in this place only briefly, for three months. These three months were enough to gather an immeasurable experience—a treasure for spiritual growth—but short enough not to make our bodies and spirits broken and emaciated. Thus, with expectant excitement and a stubborn will to live, we headed toward the new station of our destiny.

FOUR

☐

THE REAL FORCED LABOR

Our first stop was Bergen Belsen, another concentration camp that became notorious. Later, after liberation, we returned here for a longer time period. This time it was only a temporary dwelling place for us; the purpose of our staying here was, allegedly, "holiday" rest and rehab cure before we'd start working in the factory.

We were received by a young SS soldier who addressed us as *Kinder*, "children"—the *non plus ultra* of friendliness. Our "way of life" there was comfortable indeed because the daily torture of the *Appel* was omitted and our food was also quite good. We received relatively rich soups in sufficient amounts. To serve as our dwelling place, big *Zelte*, tents were erected, their floor covered with wood shavings in which, here and there, small bugs crawled—for the time being not lice. It was bad when it rained because the water penetrated the floor of our *Zelte* and the wood shavings became all wet. We washed ourselves under the open air and under the supervision of an SS sergeant. . . .

We arrived here around mid-September, and we remained inhabitants of the Bergen camp until October 5.

Next to us, but at a fair distance, was the hospital tent. After a short while poor Györgyi R. was taken there. This time a poisonous fly had stung her on the nose. At first, she did not worry about it, but by the next day her whole face was swollen. On the third day, when we visited her for the last time, it was already completely black. We knew we were seeing her for the last time. Did the sick woman take any notice of us? Did we try to give her some spiritual preparation for the great hour? I don't remember. But I remember better what happened next—and nothing will erase it from my memory.

Evening came, and the camp became quiet. I slipped under my blanket in our tent. All at once in the dark repeated moaning reached my ears from the direction of the hospital tent. I knew right away: this can only be she! Should I get up? Should I go to her? They wouldn't let me in anyway. And I could not do anything for her! Or—maybe I could. But for that my physical presence wasn't necessary.

The moaning continued uninterrupted all night. All night I did not close my eyes. It sounded as if the agonized woman's last cry for help was begging me for help! As if God, in a mysterious way, had allowed me to have some share in the suffering of the poor dying woman, and in this union I was able to give her the ultimate help. I believe that it really happened this way. I did not even pray—I just surrendered myself to these deep, dark accords, my heart pounding on the black waves of the mortal anguish of another human being.

It lasted uninterrupted until dawn. At daybreak, the moaning suddenly stopped. I knew that I was not needed any longer, and I fell asleep.

It was only a corroboration of this inner certitude when we learned the next day that Györgyi passed away indeed at that morning hour.

I believe that God who severed her young life so suddenly welcomed her to himself with mercy. And perhaps I also helped her in that a little bit. . . .

I don't remember any other particular event through these two weeks.

■ ■ ■

Again, the hour came to get up and start out. They organized a transport to one of the many war factories. Gizi, Éva, and I managed to get into it, but Franci was left out. Of course, we in no way wanted to get separated. Among great excitements—I have no idea how, up to this day—she sneaked over to us at the last minute. And so, the "foursome alliance" was able to face together, *viribus unitis,* the coming events.

We made preparations on October 5, the first Thursday of the month—that happened to be my twenty-fourth birthday, and the next day, on first Friday evening, we took off. This was again an opportunity for surrender, for the loving readiness to accept everything that was ahead of us. This night trip was gruesome! We were traveling in the usual freight wagons. But, in contrast to our transport to Auschwitz, the weather this time was not scorching hot but a bitingly chilly autumn cold. Neither were we crowded together as much as at that earlier time. All in all, it was cold, bitter cold. Our thin, striped coats did not protect us much against it, nor were we able to warm each other. We arrived at our destination at dawn freezing and sleepy—the cold did not allow us to fall asleep.

October 7, first Saturday, the location: Salzwedel, a small town between Hanover and Hamburg. This was our abode for two months, the greater part of our exile. Of course, we lived not in the town itself but in a camp outside of it, near an ammunition factory. Of this charming little town, called "the Venice of the North," we saw nothing until our liberation. We spent half of our time in the camp, the other half in the bullet factory.

Thus, we arrived broken from fatigue. We were standing freezing in the courtyard for several more hours until they took our personal data and put the barracks in order for us new arrivals. Some people-moving must have taken place to make some room for us, and that could not be done very quickly. While being registered, we received a new number and a small metal dog tag with two holes so that we could wear it on a string around our neck so that it would not get lost. And so we did. This was our number in the factory. I have preserved this tag faithfully up to this day.

At last, around noon we got so far that we received some hot coffee and could move into our barracks. There we were welcomed by big, four-storied bunks, each with a blanket. The more resourceful of us, of course, quickly took the bunks on the lowest level. As for me, as I remember, I was on the second story. Poor Franci sacrificed herself and went up to the highest level. You can imagine how we collapsed in our bed.

The next day, since it was Sunday, there was no work. We got acquainted with our immediate surroundings. The barracks were standing next to each other in a row, with the bath and restrooms at the end of the row. Winter was coming, so all these arrangements were very troublesome for us—not to mention the ice-cold water. We could not risk washing ourselves at these troughs without the danger of pneumonia, not to mention having to crawl out of bed much earlier to take the long walk. Without going to the bath, one could still linger in bed a little longer after reveille. How we aided ourselves—that will be seen later.

In the factory, work went on in two shifts. One from six in the morning until six in the evening, the other during the night hours. We even had lengthened shifts when we worked nonstop from 6:00 AM to 9:00 PM with a short break for breakfast and lunch. That meant that on such days we had the privilege of receiving soup twice.

Right on the first day, we had a great sorrow: we got separated from Gizi and Éva. They were appointed to the other shift, and so they also had to stay in the other barracks building. From this time on, we could see each other only on Sundays.

The factory work presented itself to us from its most difficult side: our group started working the night shift. After finishing our supper, we filed up in the usual five-deep ranks, and, led by the woman who was our supervisor, we took off.

From the beginning onward, our ranks consisted, besides Franci and myself, of three sisters, the Kertész girls. Two of them were unmarried, and the third one was a married woman. They were also called the "redheads," although only two of them had red hair, and the third one was a brunette. Of the three of them I liked Rózsi the most, maybe because she had my mother's name, but also because she was the gentlest of them. Their big trouble was that they did not speak German at all, not even Yiddish, and thus they were unable to communicate with our guards or with coworkers in the factory. In a foreign-language environment this was indeed a very unpleasant circumstance.

In need, we were their interpreters. Of course, we did not speak German fluently either since at home we had never thought of practicing German conversation. My knowledge of German only started blooming later, under the open air of Salzwedel. But still, we were able to understand German words, and we managed to make ourselves understood.

■ ■ ■

I was trying to guess and to inquire about the number of residents in our camp, but I could not obtain any certain figures. After our liberation, I wrote in my notes that "out of 3,000 exactly I!" But I could not say whether this figure was the normal, usual number or the number inflated by dwellers added from other camps. The first possibility cannot be excluded, since the war factory—the ammunition plant of Salzwedel—was huge indeed.

■ ■ ■

The camp was located very close to the factory, about five to ten minutes by foot. But even that was too much for us to march in our thin clothing, since we had weathered the entire winter in our camp cape. Even hosiery we received only on November 19, maybe due to the goodness of St. Elizabeth—although the first snow had already come on November 12. As a result, I carry on my legs even now the decorative spots of frostbite, which in cold weather become more faint and blue, and in warm weather swell and show all the shades of red and purple. But they don't cause any pain—and that's the main thing. All the more unpleasant were those bladder problems that manifested themselves even after our return home, as a result of catching a chill.

The human body is a very particular mechanism! The soul—the current running through this mechanism—indicates the danger, and all the organs are doing their job with stubborn perseverance. What we could not tolerate out there! As long as we had to, we took it! As Fr. Lenz remarked, "Diarrhea and pneumonia, two fatal diseases, could flourish among us!"

Trust in God and sheer willpower: these were our saviors. For the sake of God's love, I just should not become sick! No, that is out of the question!—This was the thought that dominated our minds. Whoever gets sick is lost! This inner power of resistance was decisive.

Whoever lost that also lost herself. But whoever clung to God possessed the greatest inner strength.

■ ■ ■

During the time while we were marching to our workplace or back from there, we had to keep strictly silent all the way. After all we were marching "under the cover of darkness" at dawn or in the evening, and thus we were forbidden to call to ourselves the attention of the good German citizens. And indeed, most of them did not even know about us. If someone broke the silence, the response was a slap on the face by our female supervisor. I myself also had my share of slaps, here and there. Of course, there was no possibility of excuse or explanation. "Silence!" snapped the sharp warning, followed immediately by the "measure" (a slap on the face) meted out to the one whom she found guilty.

■ ■ ■

In that improbable world in which we had been since June this factory was among the least probable phases. After all, it was here that most of us for the first time stepped over the threshold of a big, real industrial plant. And this was real indeed! The terrible reality of a bloody war! The factory produced ammunition, shells for rifles; I'm not sure whether in the entire plant or just in one part of it. In any case, that was all we saw in different phases of its production.

The *H-Halle*, the shell processing hall, a huge workshop with its dizzyingly loud machines buzzing—this sight received us when we first entered. The process of making the case started at the section called *Beiz*, or mill, where we were shoveling thick, gray, lead tips into huge machines. You can imagine them as tops of toothpaste tubes but, of course, of a much bigger size. In the machine, they were heated to very high temperatures so that they become pliable, and they exited the machines before our amazed eyes as long, sparkling, white, empty half-cylinders. Another machine cut their edges straight, and with that the preparation phase was completed. The cases then were transported to another part of the huge hall to be filled with gunpowder.

During my career as a female factory worker, I tried out just about all the lines of work, but I never got to that part of the factory. I suppose that we prisoners were not sufficiently trustworthy to handle explosives.

Then the filled cases returned to a workshop called the lacquerer. This was elegant work, easy but requiring skillful hands, and its results were elegant too: chocolate-brown-colored little things, shiny treacherous beauties—their inside was death. Once in a while one exploded.

The completed merchandise was taken to the packaging area, where they were boxed and sealed. But in between these two phases was also the sorting—this was the fifteen-hour shift during which we picked out the defective shells, the ones that were dented or had crooked edges.

This was the work process that from October 1944 until April 1945 absorbed thousands and thousands of foreign prisoners—those people considered and called subhuman—like tiny atoms.

Yet we were still human, and while our muscles were working with stubborn effort and our nerves were tightened, in our souls the persistent drive of hope and the drive "to remain human" kept vigil.

If it is possible to condense into one phrase all the events, longings, aspirations of these seven months, perhaps the phrase is this: "to remain human."

After all, we should not forget that, in general, well-educated, cultured, white-collar people with intellectual needs were thrown together here. Life, the salvaging of which was the main purpose for most of us (even if we did not all reason it through consciously), obviously meant more than mere vegetation.

To put it simply: we kept struggling to remain human!

FIVE

□

THE FREE PRISONER

Time was, even if lead-footed, progressing. And as the days and weeks were passing by, the hope of freedom shined nearer and nearer, became more and more real. One could read not only from pages of thrown-away newspapers but also from the faces of our guards that the end was near.

I must confess, even if it sounds strange, I never felt myself as being a "prisoner." The experience of inner freedom was too strong in me that no terror coming from the outside could break it down. And we had the advantage that they did not even try to touch our souls, our world of thoughts. They did not even look at us as people who had souls and a world of thoughts. We were numbers, meant only for working. *Arbeit und Maul halten!*—"Work and keep your mouth shut!"—that was our duty and our only requirement. Whatever was boiling in our heads, what was glowing in our hearts did not bother them. At least this was the case in our camp.

The quality of loyalty was never absent in me. "Obey your superiors, even the tough ones" (Titus 3:1). I could make use of it here. Of course, I do not mean to say that I agreed with the horror that was going on there and elsewhere, but I realized completely that from their ideology only such practices can originate and, at the same time, I observed also that those who were in direct contact with us were nothing more than simple servants of those in power, small screws in a monstrous machine. Which despotic system in the history of the world has not found its own army of servants? Stupidity and fear—these two sad, great powers were always at its service among people. Such and similar thoughts occupied my mind, and thanks to them, I was not surprised by anything. All the more did every little spark of goodness, which was in startling contrast to this "theoretical" pattern, make me happy.

■ ■ ■

The air-raid alarms became more and more frequent. In the camp this had no consequence for us, after all: where could have we gone? In the factory, however, our guards were afraid for their lives and thus they ordered us to move down into the air-raid shelter. This meant real joy for us—especially during night shifts. From experience, we already knew ahead of time when they would fly over us because it happened each evening at the same time, sometime between 9:00 and 10:00 PM, and it lasted about an hour. How enjoyable this "emergency rest" was during which the exhausted workers could slumber a little! Beautiful wooden contraptions that looked like benches were waiting for us in the shelter; one day one of us looked more closely and discovered the label: "DYNAMITE." Thus, we realized that we were sitting down there on wooden cases filled with dynamite and finished ammunition ready for use.

What was the most interesting for me was that not only were the Germans scared for their lives, but our people were too. What terror and wailing prevailed over some of the groups! A few of us could not even perceive why. After all, in our lives there was not much to fear for. How many times did these very same people curse life and, yet, one can see that they were afraid for their future and hopes, the better life on which they could count after the miserable present. But I believe it was the simple stir of the instinct of life in people who did not know anything better than this "vale of tears"; that is, they did not believe in anything else.

At this point it was all the same to me how the Lord God would provide. But an inner awareness, even more than that: an intuition that I would stay alive accompanied me throughout the entire time. Why and for what God would want to keep me, I did not know. I did not know it and I did not even search for it. I accepted life with love from the fatherly hands the same way as I had accepted death quietly. He knows better. . . .

■ ■ ■

Toward spring this work was already fading fast. We no longer received supplies of raw material. Of course, that did not bother us at all.

Then around the beginning of April came the first and last air raid. Because up to that time the Allied planes had flown over Salzwedel, they had never attacked us. The well-informed among us thought that this happened because of us. And this is also very likely, as after all the Allied forces had very precise information. In the factory French political prisoners were also working. Allegedly they were able to send word to their compatriots—including the information that our SS guards were planning to flee. That was when the bombing attack took place. I don't remember the day, but I know for sure that it happened on a day when we did not work. Maybe it was a Sunday. One bomb hit the factory, and another ruined the railroad station with the SS train ready to take off. For us the result was that we had to clean away the rubble, lay down rails, and do other similar projects. In these jobs, I could not participate any longer.

On April 13, planes flew over us again, and this time they dropped flyers over the camp area. At that time, we were staying "at home" because work had become impossible and futile. Our guards angrily forbade us to touch these papers, but of course they could not stop us from picking some up. The slips told us: They are COMING, let us not evacuate the camp. As if there had been any strength in us to resist, had it come to such an action! But the evacuation would have been certain death for us—the sad fate of other camps showed that. In the state in which we were at that time—emaciated, debilitated, sick, at the farthest limit of our strength— in no way would we have been able to survive such a notorious forced march. Providence, however, who knows, carried our small band in the palm of his hand. It was not we who were transported; instead they brought the dwellers of other nearby camps (such as Ravensbrück) to us. They arrived in terrible condition, those who arrived at all, and they swelled the camp to the utmost limit. But all this just zoomed by us during the last week.

We were indeed at the end of our strength. The end of the factory work was handy but, of course, our starvation did not end yet, and if the liberation had been delayed just one day, I have no idea how many of us it would have found alive in spite of our stubborn will to live. By then the destiny of the proverbial donkey, which expired just when it had got used to starvation, would had been fulfilled in us. But Someone took care of us along with the little sparrows and allowed us to live to see April 14, 1945, when, around noon, the gates of the camp were opened, and the first American soldiers entered. . . .

I had returned from the hospital to my barracks only the previous day, perhaps just so that I would be able to participate in this big event. As it soon turned out, I did not remain long among the "healthy" ones. But at that time I saw the two big sea waves swelling toward each other: the well-fed, cheerful American soldiers as they were coming into the camp, and emaciated, striped-caped skeletons caught by the irresistible breath of freedom as they were pouring out into the street. . . .

We could go without worrying, as after all we had nothing to be afraid for from the occupying forces. . . . We rather expected good things from them, and in this we were not disappointed because they were handing out with cheerful readiness and startling compassion whatever they had: cigarettes, chocolate, canned food. . . . Unfortunately, this became fatal for more than one prisoner who had been able to survive the miserable months at the camp. The stomach was unable to digest the sudden overabundant rich, fat food, which resulted in gastric catarrh and death. In the strictest sense of the word they ate themselves to death. But I learned this only later from the news.

■ ■ ■

Looking back, I see myself with Franci, as we cling to each other, walking through the gate into the city, driven by some irresistible instinct. Wherever we went, the passersby stopped, windows opened, eyes filled with tears, startled faces stared at us. We saw only then how the guileless German citizens had absolutely no idea what was going on in their immediate vicinity. They just looked dumbfounded and wailed. And we just walked and walked. . . . When, at last, we asked someone where we could find a Catholic church, we were already very near to it. Perhaps our hearts were guiding us toward it?

At noon, it was quiet in the small church, and a lone elderly lady was saying her prayers. And we—the first time after so many months—collapsed before Christ of the Eucharist. . . .

When we left the church, the old lady quickly came after us. Later I had the opportunity to get acquainted with her more closely because she also lived at the Skripaliks', my landlords. She suffered from some religious mania. But what she did then was very kind and unforgettable. After she made sure that we understood German, she said she had nothing else but that we should accept from her a scarf and a pair of gloves—and she pressed us to take a checkered, shabby cotton scarf and a pair of black knit gloves. I've kept these items for a long time as relics, as tokens of the goodwill, love, and restitution with which Germany approached us in the first hours of our freedom.

We were looking for the pastor. I can imagine what a shocking experience it was for him to meet us, but for us it was natural, since like someone dying of thirst we longed for the sacraments. It's clear that at the first possible moment we were able to we set out to satisfy our desire. This was a more urgent need for us than to wash ourselves or to bring our inhuman outward appearance into some human shape. Of course, our knowledge of German was quite poor for the "terminology" of confession, but somehow we managed it.

Thus, cleansed and light as a feather, we were suddenly in the mood to look around in the city. Our liberators gave permission for "free looting" for twenty-four hours. One can imagine the results. Wherever we went, we saw shattered show windows, broken-down doors . . . at one place a whole pile of marks . . . elsewhere sugar covered the floor. . . . We picked up some odds and ends: a pencil, an eraser. . . . These were dreamlike objects for us!

Anyway, of course, we arrived everywhere too late. But somehow our taste and conscience also protested while our eyes and stomachs, of course, represented the opposite position.

This is how we rambled around, and I don't know even today whether it was our newly regained spiritual purity or our cowardice that played a greater role in that we did not get involved in these things. One thing was sure: it was not a comforting sight at all to see these animal-like humans let loose and given free rein to their passions.

■ ■ ■

It was already toward evening that we arrived in front of a bakery. Several American soldiers came, among them a black man who asked us what we wanted. "Bread," we answered longingly. At this he simply kicked open the door and we entered into our little kingdom. All at once, this became a dreamland for us. The little house was a middle-class home, fully furnished with all comforts and with a bathroom. Its inhabitants had obviously fled. We closed the door, and from that time on, we did not care about the outside world. In the pantry there were eggs, flour, lard, sugar; in the cabinets fine ladies' underwear, hosiery. . . . All this seemed to be like a present prepared for us, or at least that's how it looked in the first moments. At that time, I did not yet know how much more it would mean for me. In the living room, there was a beautiful painting: a boat tossed about on the stormy sea. . . .

We feasted on the available supplies and lay down in the fine soft beds! But it was destined that we would not sleep that night. We started a conversation on the present situation, of future tasks, and the conversation lasted well into the morning.

At that time flu was already working in me, and the next day it broke out in full blast. During the night, I must have had high fever; I felt it although we did not have a way to take my temperature. This physical fever gave a special tone to this whole night, a particular mood to this truly GREAT night.

Because it was a great night. I could even say a life-changing night. Two souls were standing naked before themselves and God—or rather they were vacillating on the border line of their past and future destiny like the little boat on the stormy sea.

I'd been unable to reconstruct even one sentence of this exchange of thoughts, but I know exactly: we had to arrive there that night so that we'd have a chance to take account and that I could measure up the world around me, to which I said "NO" again. In essence, this was the question. Strictly speaking and at the deepest level this was what it was all about: How much was it justified and permissible what our companions did that day? Are we Christians allowed to loot other people's property for ourselves? From the property of people who perhaps had nothing to do with what happened to us? But there was more to it and deeper. How can I say it? The "Life" was calling toward us with its seductive siren voice, the "Life" that we had left, from which we were torn ten months ago: the middle-class comfort, good food, pretty clothes, culture, entertainment. . . . I don't even want to mention that the poisonous spirit of revenge was also hovering around many of us—but it did not get close to either of us.

But I felt one thing: after this stupefying lesson that God gave as a response to my theoretical acceptance of the Cross, God wanted more, expected more from me than a sinking back into what at that time I could only call "a petty, middle-class way of thinking." Behind my hot forehead sweating from fever, I unraveled all of this with cool brain and cold, hard hands. I did not want to convince my companion. I knew that this path is not for everyone. But during this night a chasm opened up between the two of us. Love and good friendship remained unchanged afterward, but the period of sisterhood was over. That, it seems, was given to us only for the time of suffering as a source of strength.

■ ■ ■

Morning came and the inner separation was followed by the outward one. Franci packed a nice full suitcase that, it seems, the inhabitants of the house could not take along, with things for the beginning of a new life: silk underwear, hosiery, some dresses, and so on. I myself took out of the pocket of my coat even the thrown-away eraser and the rest of the small items I picked up during the looting.

We stepped out into the dawn. My fever was gone. I felt wonderfully light and happy. We shook hands and took off—in two directions. Franci went back in the camp saying that she would take "home" her treasures and come back for a later Mass. I was flying with exultation toward the church. . . .

I should write this day in red letters. After ten months of fasting, after ten months of craving: Holy Mass, Holy Communion!

The authentic story of the hours following after that dropped completely from my mind. Hazily, something vaguely looms as if after church someone took me along for breakfast. . . . then as if I returned to the camp. . . . But this is not sure. What is certainly sure is that during the morning hours of the same day the sickness broke out in full blast. Along with the relaxation of the spiritual tension my physical powers also gave up. I think I fainted. In any case it became advisable to take me to the hospital—not to the camp hospital but to the city hospital of Salzwedel. And that was the greatest gift of Providence that he could give me. I can state without exaggeration that this was not only literally my life-saver but intellectually and spiritually as well.

■ ■ ■

Spiritually I perceived my stay at the hospital from the first minute as a religious retreat. "The Paradise of human goodness," I wrote about this time. The cool, white beds, the caring nurses, at their head Schwester Käthe. . . .

My fever was gone quickly, but what remained was the "marasmus"—because this word characterized best my physical state: the stubborn diarrhea that not even "plaster paste" was able to stop. The doctors were clueless.

To eat was very painful for me—but I had to eat if I wanted to stay alive. Fortunately, the good God created the potato. This was the only thing that I could tolerate—boiled in water, without anything else. This, however, I was consuming in frightening quantities. I would, after lunch, go down in the kitchen (when I was already able to walk) to ask for more.

I am thankful for this cautious nutrition, that my digestive system slowly solved the task of my returning to normal life, and I started to get stronger. During the following months, I reached the point that I was able to return home by and large in my old state of health.

■ ■ ■

A small notebook with a yellow cover. Inside, faded handwritten lines in ink pencil. . . .

I received these treasures on April 16 in the hospital, and right on the same day I started writing a journal with thirsty diligence. The good Käthe—she gave them to me; I think she probably could not even perceive what an unearthly happiness these items gave to me, these objects so commonly used in everyday life.

Allow me to quote a few of these short entries:

■ April 18, 1945, Wednesday

Magnificat! May this be the first word that I write down. And thanks and homage and praise and adoration! . . . Both sorrow for sins and hope, the new hope and condition of becoming a human being and a saint!

I have a Bible! I have a journal!—I have everything! With this I begin my little spiritual exercise in the sanatorium, if God helps me! Its method will be meditation on the scriptural text, searching for its application on my present situation.

■ April 29, Sunday

Der Krieg ist beendet! La guerre est finie! La guerra è finita! The war is ended! There are no more blood and tears and bombs and cities crushed into dust . . . or orphans, widows . . . Peace! Peace! Peace! We were waiting for it and yet it's so incredible! . . . *Deo gratias! DEO GRATIAS!*

The world, sighing with relief after six years of torments, places its joy before God. . . . It's right now that we must indeed pray and thus lend helping hands for a true, lasting, worldwide peace inspired by love and justice!

■ April 30, Monday

The joyful news proved to be premature, but it still must be only a matter of days.

Hitler is no more—I'm reciting the Divine Office of the dead for him . . . There are lilacs in my room. . . . Lilacs of May! . . .

■ May 1, Tuesday

Ave Maria! At home, the chapel of the clinic is resounding from the litany. . . . Lilacs, lilies-of-the-valley. To look at our Mother!

Now I continue the Divine Office for Mussolini. *Sic transit. . . .*[8]

■ May 7, Monday

Now the war is indeed ended. The most beautiful present for Mother's Day: peace!

8   Full quotation: *Sic transit gloria mundi.*

SIX

□

HOMEWARD BOUND

On June 13, 1945, on the Feast of St. Anthony [of Padua] (he was my mother's favorite saint; she faithfully carried in her purse his small statue, which she received when she was still a Jewish little girl; thus he counted somehow as our family patron saint), I finished the journal entry that I had started to work on, on my return home. But I soon realized that my return would "crawl slowly." From that time on I never stopped to inquire, to complain, even to demand—and to wait.

It was enough! By then I'd been away from my country for more than a year, and impatience consumed me when I thought of the life beginning at home, of the life of which I did not know anything yet, but I felt my place could only be there. —People who live according to the principle *Ubi bene, ibi patria*[9] can talk to me about "living above the concept of nation," about cosmopolitanism. After all, they told us in Bergen

9 "Wherever I'm doing well, there is my country."

that we had a good life there. The British soldiers kept repeating, "You have enough to eat and drink, we're dancing with you, what else you want?" —What do we want? Our country! "At home black bread tastes much better than white does anywhere else!"[10]

■ August 29, Wednesday

Yes, I am on my way! Finally: the relief that comes with having made a decision! Help me in this, my God! I'm doing it for you, you know it!

In ten days, on September 10, we arrived in Budapest. In the gray September morning we dispersed in silence, shivering from inner fever, looking for the traces of our loved ones. . . .

Deo gratias!!! Thanks be to God!!!

10   By Sándor Petőfi, nineteenth-century Hungarian poet.

SEVEN

☐

OUTLOOK

Yes, I was at home—along with a halfway-filled sack, a "shoulder bag" pieced together of some sheer burlap, and two gray blankets. That's what made up all my earthly possessions. During this one year I had lost everything that I ever owned, and the same happened to the country. I spent this year amid dangers of death—just like the country. But I survived—just like the country. And now I was looking for my place in a new life in the midst of completely changed circumstances—just like the whole country. "God has his intentions for you, wherever you are. . . ."[11]

The One who seemingly still wanted me saw to it that this adjustment would take place. He arranged it so that I'd find good people, friends who took me physically and spiritually under their protection. Etel's,

11 This statement seems to be a quote uttered by some anonymous friend, maybe by a spiritual director.

the maternal female friends, my spiritual fathers, my professor. . . . Even so, the acclimatization was a difficult and slow process. If I entered a home furnished according to usual "middle-class" standards, I just marveled at the sight of rugs, curtains, paintings, and the rest: What's the use of so many things? Is mere life not enough? How well I was able to sleep on the bare ground! . . .

What was even more difficult was to find the way back inside myself, that is—what was equivalent to it— my place in the world and my God-willed task.

■ ■ ■

I have been requested by people, both privately and during lectures, to speak about the experiences I had over there, outside Hungary. I did it willingly, but I realized more and more what I should have expected: They don't understand what took place. I was able to speak about the mere facts and events, and they could imagine them more or less correctly, but what was essential to me (and, I believe, also to God) remains unapproachable for the *animalis homo*,[12] for every individual who has not had the unbelievable, sweet paradox: the bliss, the happiness of suffering.

I tried to record the pure harmonies of this reality in this book in a lasting fashion, as an old debt. And now I feel like a composer, who in comparison to what had originally resonated in her mind, has put her *opus* into shaky musical notes in a very pale, very weak manner and presented it before the public. It was not from her: she has heard it from the Source of All Harmonies. And now she is pondering: is it enough, what she managed to put on paper—even so that the Heavenly Word may resound in just one soul?

But if it was not even enough for that, I don't mind. Let it then be the ascending melody of gratitude and homage to the One from whom all this came. He will surely understand it. And, out of the fertilizer of suffering, he will let germinate an even greater abundance of flowers in the heart and in the world.

Let it be!

12 See 1 Cor. 2:14. The *animalis homo,* or "natural person," is a person without supernatural help from God.

ACKNOWLEDGMENTS

My sincere thanks go to Michael O'Brien, formerly a student, later an English teacher at the Cistercian Preparatory School, Irving, Texas, who carefully edited the text and also greatly improved it by his numerous wise suggestions. Thank you, Michael! Later, Michael finished law school and today he is a lawyer.

—J.D.L., Irving, October 23, 2018,
the 62nd anniversary of the 1956 Hungarian Revolution
against the Soviet Union